NUMBERS

J. Vernon McGee

THOMAS NELSON
Since 1798

NASHVILLE DALLAS MEXICO CITY RIO DE JANEIRO

Published in Nashville, Tennessee, by Thomas Nelson, Inc

Scripture quotations are from the KING JAMES VERSION of the Bible

Library of Congress Cataloging-in-Publication Data

McGee, J. Vernon (John Vernon), 1904–1988
    [Thru the Bible with J. Vernon McGee]
    Thru the Bible commentary series / J. Vernon McGee.
      p.   cm.
    Reprint. Originally published: Thru the Bible with J. Vernon McGee. 1975.
    Includes bibliographical references.
    ISBN 0-7852-1008-3 (TR)
    ISBN 0-7852-1074-1 (NRM)
    1. Bible—Commentaries. I. Title.
BS491.2.M37   1991
220.7'7—dc20   90–41340
ISBN: 978-0-7852-0332-2   CIP

Printed in the United States

24 25 26 27 28 EPAC 15 14 13 12 11

CONTENTS

NUMBERS

PREFACE

The radio broadcasts of the Thru the Bible Radio five-year program were transcribed, edited, and published first in single-volume paperbacks to accommodate the radio audience.

There has been a minimal amount of further editing for this publication. Therefore, these messages are not the word-for-word recording of the taped messages which went out over the air. The changes were necessary to accommodate a reading audience rather than a listening audience.

These are popular messages, prepared originally for a radio audience. They should not be considered a commentary on the entire Bible in any sense of that term. These messages are devoid of any attempt to present a theological or technical commentary on the Bible. Behind these messages is a great deal of research and study in order to interpret the Bible from a popular rather than from a scholarly (and too-often boring) viewpoint.

We have definitely and deliberately attempted "to put the cookies on the bottom shelf so that the kiddies could get them."

The fact that these messages have been translated into many languages for radio broadcasting and have been received with enthusiasm reveals the need for a simple teaching of the whole Bible for the masses of the world.

I am indebted to many people and to many sources for bringing this volume into existence. I should express my especial thanks to my secretary, Gertrude Cutler, who supervised the editorial work; to Dr. Elliott R. Cole, my associate, who handled all the detailed work with the publishers; and finally, to my wife Ruth for tenaciously encouraging me from the beginning to put my notes and messages into printed form.

Solomon wrote, ". . . of making many books there is no end; and much study is a weariness of the flesh" (Eccl. 12:12). On a sea of books that flood the marketplace, we launch this series of THRU THE BIBLE with the hope that it might draw many to the one Book, *The Bible.*

J. VERNON McGEE

The Book of

NUMBERS

INTRODUCTION

The Book of Numbers, called *Arithmoi* (meaning "Arithmetic") in the Septuagint, gets its name from the census in chapters 1 and 26. Numbers takes up the story where Exodus left off It is the fourth book of the Pentateuch.

You will recall that in Genesis, the first book of the Pentateuch, we have the creation and fall of man and many beginnings. We have the beginning of Israel—not a nation yet, but a growing family that migrates down to Egypt to escape extinction by famine

In Exodus we find the family becoming a nation in Egypt. We see them in slavery by the brick kilns of Egypt; then we see God delivering them by the hand of Moses and bringing them through the wilderness as far as Mount Sinai.

In the Book of Leviticus we see the children of Israel marking time at Mount Sinai while God gives the Law and the tabernacle. God calls them to Himself and tells them how to come

In the Book of Numbers we see the children of Israel depart from Mount Sinai and march to Kadesh-barnea. After their failure at Kadesh-barnea, they began to wander until that generation died in the wilderness. The years of wandering were a veritable saga of suffering, a trek of tragedy, and a story of straying.

"Pilgrim's Progress" is an apt theme for this book Here we find the walking, wandering, working, warring, witnessing, and worshiping of God's pilgrims. It is a handbook for pilgrims in this world. In the words of the hymnwriter, "Chart and compass come from Thee." This is a road map for the wilderness of this world.

This book is helpful for us today. The lessons which the children of Israel had to learn are the lessons that you and I will need to learn, which is the reason God recorded this history for you and me. "For whatsoever things were written aforetime were written for our learning, that we through patience and comfort of the scriptures might have hope" (Rom. 15:4).

"Now all these things happened unto them for ensamples: and they are written for our admonition, upon whom the ends of the world are come" (1 Cor. 10:11).

"These all died in faith, not having received the promises, but having seen them afar off, and were persuaded of them, and embraced them, and confessed that they were strangers and pilgrims on the earth" (Heb. 11:13).

"Dearly beloved, I beseech you as strangers and pilgrims, abstain from fleshly lusts, which war against the soul" (1 Pet. 2:11).

"I have given them thy word; and the world hath hated them, because they are not of the world, even as I am not of the world. I pray not that thou shouldest take them out of the world, but that thou shouldest keep them from the evil" (John 17:14–15).

The first five books of the Bible, called the Pentateuch (since *pentateuch* means "five books"), were written by Moses. They are identified in Scripture as the Law. Although the Mosaic authorship has been questioned, it is affirmed by conservative scholars and confirmed by archaeology. Bible believers unanimously accept the Mosaic authorship.

It is interesting to note that the distance from Mount Sinai to Kadesh-barnea was from 150 to 200 miles—a journey, in that time, of eleven days (Deut. 1:2). The Israelites spent thirty days at Kibroth. They spent forty years on a journey that should have taken forty days because their walking was turned to wandering. Since they refused to go into the land, they did not advance an inch after Kadesh-barnea. At the end of their wanderings they came back to the same place, Kadesh-barnea. What was the reason? Unbelief.

Between the census in the first chapter and the census in the twenty-sixth chapter, we find a divine history of the wanderings of the Israelites in the wilderness for about thirty-eight years and ten months, commencing with the first movement of the camp after the tabernacle was reared.

A comparison of the two sets of census figures will show that their number was decimated. Numbers 1:46 says there were 603,550 fighting men. Numbers 26:51 states that there were 601,730 fighting men. This represents a loss of 1,820 fighting men. God's command was for them to be fruitful and multiply, but they were losing instead of gaining during the years in the wilderness.

The census helps us to ascertain the number that had come out of Egypt. I am giving to you the estimate of Dr. Melvin Grove Kyle, who was a great Egyptologist and one of the editors of the *International Standard Bible Encyclopedia* and also, at one time, editor on the staff of *The National Geographic*. He was a great man and a great archaeologist—and as dull as any lecturer can be. However, a person could get a wealth of information if he would make the effort to listen to him. I must say that I found him intensely interesting. Dr. Kyle figured that with about 600,000 fighting men there would be approximately 400,000 women. He set a figure at 200,000 senior citizens and 800,000 children. Then there was a mixed multitude that followed, which he estimated to be about 100,000. This gives a total estimate of 2,100,000 people, which does not include the tribe of Levi. Between 2,000,000 and 3,000,000 would be the number who came out of the land of Egypt!

Included in this book are three illustrations that are helpful in this study. Two of them show the tabernacle and the way the children of Israel camped around it. The other illustration shows the order by which they marched.

Don't think for a moment that this was a mob going through the wilderness helter-skelter. No group ever marched more orderly than this group. As we study this, I am sure you will be impressed by the way God insisted upon the order of this camp.

This is God's method. To the church He said, "Let all things be done decently and in order" (1 Cor. 14:40). He is a God of order. Have you ever pulled aside the petals of a rose and looked deeply into it? He put the rose together nicely, didn't He? Have you noticed the way He shaped a tree? Have you noted the orderly arrangement of every fruit and vegetable you pick up? Have you observed the orderliness of this universe? Things are not flying around, bumping into each other. There is plenty of space to maneuver because the Lord has arranged it so. We live in a remarkable universe which reveals a God of power and a God of order. The psalmist said, "The fool hath said in his heart, There is no God . . ." (Ps. 14:1). Nobody but a fool could be an atheist. This universe shouts out the message. The order of the universe evidences it. The power of this tremendous universe reveals that there is a Person in control of it. Not only does it reveal a Person, but it reveals His genius.

OUTLINE

I. **Fitting out the Nation Israel for Wilderness March, Chapters 1—8**
  A. Order of the Camp, Chapters 1—4
    1. First Census, Chapter 1
    2. Standards and Positions of 12 Tribes on Wilderness March, Chapter 2
    3. Census, Position, and Service of Levites on Wilderness March, Chapter 3
    4. Service of Levites about the Tabernacle, Chapter 4
  B. Cleansing the Camp, Chapters 5—8
    1. Restitution and Jealousy Offering, Chapter 5
    2. Vow of the Nazarite, Chapter 6
    3. Gifts of the Princes, Chapter 7
    4. Light of Lampstand and Laver for Levites, Chapter 8

II. **Forward March!, Chapters 9—10**
  A. Passover and Covering Cloud, Chapter 9
  B. Order of March, Chapter 10

III **From Sinai to Kadesh-barnea, Chapters 11—12**
  A. Complaining and Murmuring of People Displeasing to the Lord, Chapter 11
  B. Jealousy of Miriam and Aaron; Judgment of Miriam, Chapter 12

IV. **Failure at Kadesh-barnea, Chapters 13—14**
  A. Spies Chosen and Sent into Land of Canaan, Chapter 13
  B. Israel Refuses to Enter Because of Unbelief, Chapter 14

V. **Faltering, Fumbling, and Fussing through the Wilderness, Chapters 15—25**
  A. God's Blessing Delayed; His Purpose Not Destroyed, Chapter 15

CHAPTER 1

THEME: The first census

And the LORD spake unto Moses in the wilderness of Sinai, in the tabernacle of the congregation, on the first
day of the second month, in the second year after they
were come out of the land of Egypt, saying [Num. 1:1].

THE FIRST CENSUS

God spoke to Moses in the wilderness, but He spoke from the tabernacle. The tabernacle was in the wilderness. Just so, the church
today is in the world. The Lord Jesus prayed, "I pray not that thou
shouldest take them out of the world, but that thou shouldest keep
them from the evil" (John 17:15). The church is in the world.

God spoke from the tabernacle. The building of God today is made
of flesh and blood, true believers who compose what we call the
church. "Now therefore ye are no more strangers and foreigners, but
fellow-citizens with the saints, and of the household of God; And are
built upon the foundation of the apostles and prophets, Jesus Christ
himself being the chief corner stone; In whom all the building fitly
framed together groweth unto an holy temple in the LORD: In whom ye
also are builded together for an habitation of God through the Spirit"
(Eph. 2:19–22). This church is made up of people who ". . . are his
workmanship, created in Christ Jesus unto good works, which God
hath before ordained that we should walk in them" (Eph. 2:10).

Take ye the sum of all the congregation of the children of
Israel, after their families, by the house of their fathers,
with the number of their names, every male by their
polls;

From twenty years old and upward, all that are able to go forth to war in Israel: thou and Aaron shall number them by their armies [Num. 1:2-3].

The children of Israel are to be numbered, and they are to be numbered for the purpose of building up an army. An army is for warfare. As slaves in the land of Egypt, God fought for them; they were not asked to fight. Now that they have been brought out of Egypt into the wilderness, they are to fight their enemies. And their enemies are out there waiting for them.

May I say that you and I who are believers living in this world have enemies also. These enemies are quite real, by the way. Again let me refer back to the Epistle to the Ephesians where we are told about the warfare of believers in this world today. "Finally, my brethren, be strong in the Lord, and in the power of his might. Put on the whole armour of God, that ye may be able to stand against the wiles of the devil. For we wrestle not against flesh and blood, but against principalities, against powers, against the rulers of the darkness of this world, against spiritual wickedness in high places" (Eph. 6:10-12).

God has saved us by His infinite, marvelous, wonderful grace. But you and I are in a world that is wicked and rough. Like the children of Israel out in the wilderness, we are in the wilderness of this world, which is full of sin. Although God has *saved* us by His marvelous grace, we have an enemy to fight. Paul wrote this to a young preacher, "Thou therefore endure hardness, as a good soldier of Jesus Christ" (2 Tim. 2:3). Again, he tells him, "Fight the good fight of faith, lay hold on eternal life, whereunto thou art also called . . ." (1 Tim. 6:12).

Now for the first time the Israelites hear of war. In this book we will find wars and trumpets, battles and giants—all of that. You and I live in that kind of world yet today.

In our day some folk seem to think that all one must do is say, "Peace," and there will be peace. They talk about making love and not war. Yet, they cause dissension and trouble while they talk about peace! They know nothing about true peace. They don't seem to un derstand that we live in a big, bad world, that there are some bad folk around us, and that there will be fights and wars whether we like it or not. That is one of the terrible things about our world.

And with you there shall be a man of every tribe; every one head of the house of his fathers [Num. 1:4].

The way this book starts off here with this census doesn't sound exactly thrilling. It's not like a mystery story on television. One would think we have here fifty-four verses of unnecessary details which are quite boring, but we need to remember that these details were important to God. If we will see the great truths that are here, we will find it thrilling for us.

First of all, we see that God is interested in the individuals. Mass movements have their place and play their role, but God is interested in redeemed individuals. He is interested in every individual.

Moses and Aaron were to take a census and they were to have one assistant from each tribe. The names of these assistants are given here, which are too monotonous to quote, yet they reveal that every name there was important to God and has meaning. If one understands the Hebrew meaning of the names, it will give a wonderful message.

And these are the names of the men that shall stand with you; of the tribe of Reuben; Elizur the son of Shedeur [Num. 1:5].

That doesn't sound very interesting or thrilling, but let me explain it. Reuben was the eldest son of Jacob, and he was set aside. We are told, "Reuben, thou art my firstborn, my might, and the beginning of my strength, the excellency of dignity, and the excellency of power: Unstable as water, thou shalt not excel; because thou wentest up to thy father's bed; then defiledst thou it: he went up to my couch" (Gen. 49:3–4). Reuben—unstable as water.

Now the man chosen out of this tribe was to be a different kind of man. Elizur, the son of Shedeur, was the man. *Elizur* means "My God is a rock" and *Shedeur* means "The Almighty is a fire." I like that

This man Elizur, "My God is a rock," may belong to a tribe that is unstable as water, but he knows a Rock that is stable. He reminds me of the little Scottish lady who said, "I may tremble on the Rock, but the Rock never trembles under me." Remember that they had sung in the song of Moses that God was their Rock. This fellow had learned that. He knew that God is a Rock in a weary land. He is the foundation Rock for us to rest on also. It is wonderful to know, my friend, that you may be an unstable person and come from an unstable family, but there is a Rock for you. "My God is a Rock."

> And they assembled all the congregation together on the first day of the second month, and they declared their pedigrees after their families, by the house of their fathers, according to the number of the names, from twenty years old and upward, by their polls [Num. 1:18].

Why did they declare their pedigree? Why are pedigrees so important in the Word of God? They serve a threefold purpose.

1. They were interesting and beneficial to those who were concerned. It's well to know something of your ancestry, what kind of stock you came from.

2. The reason some names and genealogies are omitted in the Bible and others are recorded is because it was important to preserve the genealogy of Jesus Christ. We saw in our study of Genesis how the rejected line was given first and then dropped and forgotten. Then the genealogical line which would lead to the Lord Jesus is given, and this line is followed all the way through the Scriptures.

The New Testament opens with a genealogy, and the whole New Testament stands or falls on the accuracy of that genealogy. This genealogy was kept on record, and probably was open on display, in the temple of that day. Probably the enemy checked it many times, hoping to find that Jesus did not have the legal right to the throne of David. It is interesting that the accuracy of the genealogy of Jesus Christ was never questioned by His enemies.

3 God forbade intermarriage, and a true Israelite had to be able to

declare his pedigree. They were the beneficiaries of the covenant made to Abraham. Also the genealogy was necessary to determine who was eligible for the priesthood. We find an example of this in the Book of Nehemiah. "And of the priests: the children of Habaiah, the children of Koz, the children of Barzillai, which took one of the daughters of Barzillai the Gileadite to wife, and was called after their name. These sought their register among those that were reckoned by genealogy, but it was not found: therefore were they, as polluted, put from the priesthood" (Neh. 7:63–64). Levites who could not declare their genealogy were put out of the priesthood.

There is a message in all of this for us today. Can you imagine a young man of that day being called up and asked, "Are you an Israelite?" If he answered, "Well, I hope I'm an Israelite, but I can't be sure until I die," what do you think would have happened? They would have pushed him aside! Suppose another young man stepped up and they asked, "Are you an Israelite?" What do you think they would have done to him if he answered, "Well, I try to be an Israelite, I'm working real hard at it, and I hope to become one"? Would that have been acceptable? Do you see how important it was for them to declare that they were Israelites? Each one must know that he was the son of Abraham.

Now I have a question for you—a quite personal question. Can you declare your pedigree as a Christian? If you don't know whether you can or not, may I say to you that you had better be able to declare it. Listen to this: "Beloved, now are we the sons of God, and it doth not yet appear what we shall be: but we know that, when he shall appear, we shall be like him; for we shall see him as he is" (1 John 3:2). Can you say that, my friend?

How can you become a son of God? "For ye are all the children of God by faith in Christ Jesus" (Gal. 3:26). There is no other way. You become a son of God by faith in Christ Jesus. "But as many as received him, [the Lord Jesus], to them gave he power to become the sons of God, even to them that believe on his name" (John 1:12). The authority to become the sons of God is given to those who do no more nor less than simply believe in His name.

And our genealogy is important! If we are a true child of God through faith in Christ, then we are heirs of God and joint heirs of Christ! "And if ye be Christ's, then are ye Abraham's seed, and heirs according to the promise" (Gal. 3:29). "For as many as are led by the Spirit of God, they are the sons of God. For ye have not received the spirit of bondage again to fear; but ye have received the Spirit of adoption, whereby we cry, Abba, Father. The Spirit itself beareth witness with our spirit, that we are the children of God: And if children, then heirs; heirs of God, and joint-heirs with Christ; if so be that we suffer with him, that we may be also glorified together" (Rom. 8:14–17).

You can *know* it. You can be born again through the blood of Christ and so be a member of the family of God. That is the only way! In this wilderness journey today, you must know who you are! You must know that you are a child of God. If you are not sure of that, you ought to make sure of it and you *can* make sure of it. How can you be sure? By taking God at His Word. It is not what you think or what you feel; He says that if you put your trust in Christ, you are His child. You can rest on the Word of God.

Here we are given the twelve tribes of Israel and the numbers in each tribe. If you were to take an adding machine and go through this chapter, you would find that it is accurate.

> **Those that were numbered of them, even of the tribe of Reuben, were forty and six thousand and five hundred.**

> **Those that were numbered of them, even of the tribe of Simeon, were fifty and nine thousand and three hundred [Num. 1:21, 23].**

So it goes down the list until verse 46.

> **Even all they that were numbered were six hundred thousand and three thousand and five hundred and fifty [Num. 1:46].**

Now we will notice that the Levites were not numbered.

> **But the Levites after the tribe of their fathers were not numbered among them**

For the LORD had spoken unto Moses, saying,

Only thou shalt not number the tribe of Levi, neither take the sum of them among the children of Israel:

But thou shalt appoint the Levites over the tabernacle of testimony, and over all the vessels thereof, and over all things that belong to it: they shall bear the tabernacle, and all the vessels thereof; and they shall minister unto it, and shall encamp round about the tabernacle [Num. 1:47–50].

The reason they were not numbered for warfare was that they had full charge of the tabernacle. They would put it up in the evening when

HOW ISRAEL ENCAMPED ON WILDERNESS MARCH
CHART OF CAMP

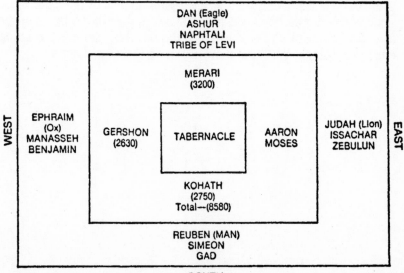

NORTH
12 Tribes of Israel

DAN (Eagle)
ASHUR
NAPHTALI
TRIBE OF LEVI

MERARI
(3200)

WEST

EPHRAIM
(Ox)
MANASSEH
BENJAMIN

GERSHON
(2630)

TABERNACLE

AARON
MOSES

JUDAH (Lion)
ISSACHAR
ZEBULUN

EAST

KOHATH
(2750)
Total—(8580)

REUBEN (MAN)
SIMEON
GAD

SOUTH

they came into camp, and they would take it down whenever they
were ready to march.

> And when the tabernacle setteth forward, the Levites
> shall take it down: and when the tabernacle is to be
> pitched, the Levites shall set it up: and the stranger that
> cometh nigh shall be put to death.
>
> And the children of Israel shall pitch their tents, every
> man by his own camp, and every man by his own stan-
> dard, throughout their hosts.
>
> But the Levites shall pitch round about the tabernacle of
> testimony, that there be no wrath upon the congregation
> of the children of Israel: and the Levites shall keep the
> charge of the tabernacle of testimony [Num. 1:51–53].

The children of Israel had to know who they were, hence the genealogy. It was also important that each of them should know where he
belonged. He had a definite place assigned to him in the camp. The
same is true for us. We need to know our pedigree, the fact that we
belong to the family of God as His children. And, we need to know
where we belong. We'll see more of this in the next chapter.

CHAPTER 2

THEME: The arrangement of the camp

In chapter 1 we learned about the census. Each Israelite had to know who he was. He also had to know where he belonged. During all these years in the wilderness, the camp positions and the order of their marching were orderly and according to God's direction.

We are told that they raised standards over their camps. These were banners that were put up over them. Just what was on these banners? Let me quote to you from two great scholars of the Old Testament, Keil and Delitzsch, in their *Commentary on the Pentateuch,* Volume III: "Neither the Mosaic law, nor the Old Testament generally gives us any intimation as to the form or character of the standard (*deqhel*). According to rabbinical tradition, the standard of Judah bore the figure of a lion, that of Reuben the likeness of a man, or of a man's head, that of Ephraim the figure of an ox, and that of Dan the figure of an eagle; so that the four living creatures united in the cherubic forms described by Ezekiel were represented upon these four standards."

I don't want to make too much of that because there is a danger in trying to read too much into it. There are people who go so far as to find in their arrangement about the camp a picture of the way the stars are arranged in heaven, the signs of the Zodiac! Also there are people who try to find the gospel written in the stars or try to find their future written in the stars. Shakespeare said, "It's not in our stars but in ourselves that we are underlings." Our problem is within ourselves, not up yonder in the stars. We won't find the gospel in the stars; we find it in the Word of God. Without the Word of God we would not suspect that the gospel was in the stars. Mankind is not without excuse because they could read the gospel in the stars but because all creation reveals God's eternal power and Godhead. Whether the standards bore a name or emblem is unimportant, and we know that tradition is not always accurate.

THE ARRANGEMENT OF THE CAMP

And the LORD spake unto Moses and unto Aaron, saying,

Every man of the children of Israel shall pitch by his own standard, with the ensign of their father's house: far off about the tabernacle of the congregation shall they pitch.

And on the east side toward the rising of the sun shall they of the standard of the camp of Judah pitch throughout their armies: and Nahshon the son of Amminadab shall be captain of the children of Judah [Num. 2:1–3].

Notice that they all camp in reference to the tabernacle. The tabernacle would be placed in the camp and then the children of Israel would camp around it. They would put up their standards to mark their place in the camp.

On the east side was Judah. The tribe of Issachar (v. 5) and the tribe of Zebulun (v. 7) camped with Judah under the same standard. If the emblem on that standard was a lion, then when these three tribes saw the standard with the lion, they knew where they belonged.

On the south side shall be the standard of the camp of Reuben according to their armies: and the captain of the children of Reuben shall be Elizur the son of Shedeur [Num. 2:10].

The tribe of Reuben was on the south side and Simeon (v. 12) and Gad (v 14) camped with Reuben.

On the west side shall be the standard of the camp of Ephraim according to their armies: and the captain of the sons of Ephraim shall be Elishama the son of Ammihud [Num. 2:18].

On the west the tribes of Manasseh (v. 20) and Benjamin (v. 22) camped with Ephraim under his emblem.

> **The standard of the camp of Dan shall be on the north side by their armies: and the captain of the children of Dan shall be Ahiezer the son of Ammishaddai [Num. 2:25].**

The tribes of Asher (v. 27) and Naphtali (v. 29) camped with Dan under his standard.

The children of Israel camped in an orderly way. Each family in each tribe knew where it belonged in that tribe.

> **But the Levites were not numbered among the children of Israel; as the Lord commanded Moses.**

> **And the children of Israel did according to all that the Lord commanded Moses: so they pitched by their standards, and so they set forward, every one after their families, according to the house of their fathers [Num. 2:33–34].**

We have learned now that they must know who they were and where they belonged. They must know their pedigree in order to know their place in the camp. They could not go to war unless they were sure of their position.

Just so, Christian warfare is not carried on in the realm of doubts and fears but in the clear light of a sure salvation. Our enemies today are the world, the flesh, and the devil. My friend, they will overcome you if you are not sure of your salvation.

Every person in the church of the Lord Jesus Christ has a God-appointed place. All service in the church is to be directed by the Holy Spirit. We are told that by one Spirit we are all baptized into one body. When you were put into the body, you were put in as a member. "For as the body is one, and hath many members, and all the members of that one body, being many, are one body: so also is Christ. For by one Spirit are we all baptized into one body, whether we be Jews or Gentiles, whether we be bond or free; and have been all made to drink into one Spirit. For the body is not one member, but many" (1 Cor. 12:12–14).

When He puts you into that body, He puts you there to serve. Every believer has a gift. You have a gift. The exercise of that gift is your Christian service.

There are many members of the human body and each has its function. There are over 20 bones in the foot alone. So in the body of Christ there are many gifts and each of us is to exercise his gift. You and I are to find out what our gift is. I believe that God rewards His own by the exercise of that gift. Although the Holy Spirit divides to every man severally as He wills, I do believe that 1 Corinthians 12:31 indicates we can pray and covet the best gifts. As a young man, I heard Dr. Ironside teach the Bible, and I asked God to let me teach like he taught. God heard and answered my prayer in a wonderful way. Although I can't teach like he did, God has permitted me to have a teaching ministry which I wanted and asked Him for. I think that we may covet earnestly the best gifts, but recognize this is all under the sovereign control of the Holy Spirit.

Remember Dorcas? She made clothes. You remember that when she died, they called in Simon Peter and the widows showed him the clothes Dorcas had made for them. Simon Peter probably said, "We had better raise this woman from the dead. The church needs her!" And God raised her from the dead.

Friend, you ought to find your place in the camp. Are you usurping another's place? Are you occupying a place in the church that you really can't fill and that belongs to someone else? We ought to encourage each member of our church to find his place, and that should hearten the humblest member of the church. You have a gift and God wants you to exercise it. Don't try to do someone else's job. You do what God has called you to do.

CHAPTER 3

THEME: Aaron and Moses; tribe of Levi given to Aaron; three families of Levi; census of firstborn of all Israel

A s we come to the third chapter, we can see that God is preparing the children of Israel for the wilderness march. First of all, there must be the order of the camp. We have seen that there was a census so that the men of war might be chosen. The people needed to be certain who they were, and to have the assurance that they were sons of Abraham. Then they needed the standards for the order of the camp so they would know where they belonged.

Chapter 3 will give us a look at the tribe of Levi and what they are to do. This is the tribe that had the oversight of the tabernacle. Although they were not included in the first census, a census is taken of them separately so that they may be assigned to a definite position in the camp.

AARON AND MOSES

These also are the generations of Aaron and Moses in the day that the LORD spake with Moses in mount Sinai.

And these are the names of the sons of Aaron; Nadab the firstborn, and Abihu, Eleazar, and Ithamar.

These are the names of the sons of Aaron, the priests which were anointed, whom he consecrated to minister in the priest's office.

And Nadab and Abihu died before the LORD, when they offered strange fire before the LORD, in the wilderness of Sinai, and they had no children: and Eleazar and Ithamar ministered in the priest's office in the sight of Aaron their father [Num. 3:1–4].

First, we are given the family of Aaron and of Moses. What we have here confirms the record that was given in the Book of Leviticus. Nadab and Abihu were destroyed because they intruded into the high priest's office, which they should not have done.

TRIBE OF LEVI GIVEN TO AARON

And the Lord spake unto Moses, saying,

Bring the tribe of Levi near, and present them before Aaron the priest, that they may minister unto him.

And they shall keep his charge, and the charge of the whole congregation before the tabernacle of the congregation, to do the service of the tabernacle [Num. 3:5–7].

The tribe of Levi was given to the high priest, Aaron, to assist him. You and I, in the church as believers, are a priesthood of believers. As such, we have been given to our Great High Priest. Listen to the Lord Jesus in His high-priestly prayer: "I have manifested thy name unto the men which thou gavest me out of the world: thine they were, and thou gavest them me; and they have kept thy word" (John 17:6). Believers, which collectively are called the church, have been given to the Lord Jesus. This entire chapter records His wonderful prayer for us. We have been given as a love gift from the Father to the Son. Some of us may feel that He didn't get very much. We need to remember that it is not what we are now, but what He is going to make out of us, that is important.

This giving of the Levites to Aaron is mentioned again.

And thou shalt give the Levites unto Aaron and to his sons: they are wholly given unto him out of the children of Israel [Num. 3:9].

Now the reason is stated:

> And I, behold, I have taken the Levites from among the children of Israel instead of all the firstborn that openeth the matrix among the children of Israel: therefore the Levites shall be mine;
>
> Because all the firstborn are mine; for on the day that I smote all the firstborn in the land of Egypt I hallowed unto me all the firstborn in Israel, both man and beast: mine shall they be: I am the Lord [Num. 3:12–13].

That was the way God put it back there. I think today He still asks every family to give Him not only our possessions but to give Him the members of our household. Have you dedicated your own to the Lord? Have you turned them over to Him? It is a wonderful thing to be able to dedicate your own to Him.

The firstborn belongs to the Lord. That doesn't mean that he must go into the ministry, but he was to be redeemed to show that he belonged to God. In Israel, instead of taking the firstborn from each tribe, God had them numbered; and He took the tribe of Levi.

THREE FAMILIES OF LEVI

> And the Lord spake unto Moses in the wilderness of Sinai, saying,
>
> Number the children of Levi after the house of their fathers, by their families: every male from a month old and upward shalt thou number them.
>
> And Moses numbered them according to the word of the Lord, as he was commanded.
>
> And these were the sons of Levi by their names; Gershon, and Kohath, and Merari [Num. 3:14–17].

There were three families in the tribe of Levi, families of his three sons: Gershon, Kohath, and Merari.

The family of Gershon is counted. They are told to pitch their tents behind the tabernacle westward. Their assignment was to take care of the curtains, coverings and cords of the tabernacle (vv. 21–26).

The family of Kohath is counted. They are to pitch on the side of the tabernacle southward. Their assignment is to be in charge of the articles of furniture of the tabernacle (vv. 27–32).

The family of Merari is counted. They are to pitch on the side of the tabernacle northward. Their assignment is to be in charge of the boards, bars, pillars, sockets, and vessels of the tabernacle (vv. 33–37).

We can now visualize the pattern of Israel encamped on the wilderness march. The tabernacle formed a rectangle in the center of the camp. Another rectangle was formed around the tabernacle by the camps of the Levites. Still another, larger rectangle was formed around that by the camps of the twelve tribes. The tabernacle was always set with the door to the east. Aaron and Moses with their families camped before the door of the tabernacle on the east side. Merari was on the north, Gershon on the west, Kohath on the south. These formed the rectangle surrounding the tabernacle. Then beyond this were the camps of Judah, Issachar, Zebulun on the east; Dan, Ashur, Naphthali on the north; Ephraim, Manasseh, Benjamin on the west; Reuben, Simeon, and Gad on the south.

> **All that were numbered of the Levites, which Moses and Aaron numbered at the commandment of the LORD, throughout their families, all the males from a month old and upward, were twenty and two thousand [Num. 3:39].**

CENSUS OF FIRSTBORN OF ALL ISRAEL

And the LORD said unto Moses, Number all the firstborn of the males of the children of Israel from a month old and upward, and take the number of their names.

And thou shalt take the Levites for me (I am the LORD) instead of all the firstborn among the children of Israel; and the cattle of the Levites instead of all the firstlings among the cattle of the children of Israel [Num. 3:40–41].

So Moses numbered all the firstborn among the children of Israel and found there were 22,273 males from a month old and upward who were the firstborn. This meant there were 273 more firstborn males than there were Levites; so this additional number was to be redeemed with five shekels apiece, and this was to be given to Aaron and his sons.

To the critic of the Bible there appears in this chapter contradictions in the numbers given. Rather than to devote space to a study of this kind, I refer the interested reader to the very fine work done by Keil and Delitzsch in the third volume of their *Commentary on the Old Testament*.

CHAPTER 4

THEME: Who is to serve; the order of service

The three families of the tribe of Levi had service to perform about the tabernacle. This chapter tells us who is to serve, what was the order of their service, and how many there were in the tribe who served.

WHO IS TO SERVE

And the LORD spake unto Moses and unto Aaron, saying,

Take the sum of the sons of Kohath from among the sons of Levi, after their families, by the house of their fathers,

From thirty years old and upward even until fifty years old, all that enter into the host, to do the work in the tabernacle of the congregation [Num. 4:1-3].

The prime of life for the Levites was from thirty to fifty years. Those were the years they were to serve.

THE ORDER OF SERVICE

This shall be the service of the sons of Kohath in the tabernacle of the congregation, about the most holy things:

And when the camp setteth forward, Aaron shall come, and his sons, and they shall take down the covering veil, and cover the ark of testimony with it:

And shall put thereon the covering of badgers' skins, and shall spread over it a cloth wholly of blue, and shall put in the staves thereof.

> And when Aaron and his sons have made an end of covering the sanctuary, and all the vessels of the sanctuary, as the camp is to set forward; after that, the sons of Kohath shall come to bear it: but they shall not touch any holy thing, lest they die. These things are the burden of the sons of Kohath in the tabernacle of the congregation [Num. 4:4–6, 15].

The only ones who ever saw the articles that belonged in the Holy of Holies—the ark and the mercy seat—were Aaron and his sons. Those articles were carefully covered by Aaron and his sons before the Kohathites came to carry them.

> This is the service of the families of the Gershonites, to serve, and for burdens:

> And they shall bear the curtains of the tabernacle, and the tabernacle of the congregation, his covering, and the covering of the badgers' skins that is above upon it, and the hanging for the door of the tabernacle of the congregation [Num. 4:24–25].

It goes on to list some of the other hangings and cords which were the responsibility of the families of Gershon.

> As for the sons of Merari . . .

> And this is the charge of their burden, according to all their service in the tabernacle of the congregation; the boards of the tabernacle, and the bars thereof, and the pillars thereof, and sockets thereof,

> And the pillars of the court round about, and their sockets, and their pins, and their cords, with all their instruments, and with all their service: and by name ye shall reckon the instruments of the charge of their burden [Num. 4:29, 31–32].

Merari carried the heavy articles, the pillars and the boards and the bars; the Kohathites carried the articles of furniture, Gershon, it would seem, had the easiest job carrying the curtains and coverings and cords.

I'd like for you to get a picture of what happened when they moved. When Moses and Aaron would come out of the tabernacle in the morning, they didn't need to talk things over. Moses didn't say, "Well, let's have a meeting of the board of elders or the board of deacons, and let's find out whether or not we should march today." They didn't depend on that type of thing. They watched to see if the pillar of cloud lifted from off the tabernacle. If it lifted, it meant that they were to march. If it did not lift, it meant that they were to stay in camp that day. Moses and Aaron simply had to watch and follow the leading that the Spirit of God gave them, for that pillar of cloud represented the Spirit of God.

The child of God should be led like that today. Not that we see a visible pillar of cloud, but we should be led by the same Spirit of God. "For as many as are led by the Spirit of God, they are the sons of God" (Rom. 8:14). The Spirit of God wants to lead the sons of God.

When the pillar of cloud lifted, immediately Aaron and his sons went into the Holy Place, and they went first to the veil. You will remember that on the other side of the veil, in the Holy of Holies, was the ark and the mercy seat. I believe that the ark and the mercy seat were put up against the veil, not against the back wall. This means that when the high priest went into the Holy of Holies, he turned around and faced east as he sprinkled the blood on the mercy seat. The high priest did that on one day of the year only. On this day of moving they did not go inside the veil. The veil was held up by rings and the high priest would let it down, and then drop the veil down over the mercy seat and the ark. Then they would put the linen cloth around it and its other coverings, and finally they would put around it the outside cover of the tabernacle. When that was concluded, and all the vessels were wrapped, the Kohathites were permitted to come in. There were staves that fit into the rings on all of these articles of furniture. The Kohathites would come in and pick up the furniture by these staves and carry it out. The priests who carried the ark would lead the way out to the front and would wait for the pillar of cloud to guide them.

We will see their marching order in a later chapter.

In the evening, it must have been a thrilling sight to see them set up a new camp. Every man knew what he was to do. Every man was carrying his particular part of the tabernacle and had been carrying it during the day's march. When they set up camp, the very first thing that was put down was the ark. The whole camp was arranged according to that. The Kohathites carrying the other articles of furniture would put them down in their relation to the ark, and then the boards and the curtains were set up around them. In other words, the furniture was put in first. Now that's not the way we build a house today, but remember this was designed for a march and it had to be mobile.

Each man had his assignment. I'm of the opinion that the camp went up in a hurry, and I mean in a hurry. I think that within about thirty minutes of the time they came to rest and the ark was put down, the tabernacle was ready to be used.

Let me illustrate this. In my first pastorate in Nashville, Tennessee, I was single and I spent a lot of time with the young people. When the circus would come to town, we would go out to the railroad yards to be there when the circus arrived at two o'clock in the morning. You could hear the animals cry, but there was no other sound. They would put the cars on the side track, and the minute those cars came to a standstill, a whole army of men would come out of those cars. The train would not have been stopped more than five minutes before the wagons were rolling off the flat cars; the circus was unloaded and moving out to the circus grounds.

A cook tent would be erected and many of the roustabouts would have coffee and breakfast while another crew would put up the big tent, the big top; then this crew would come in for breakfast while the other workers would go out to put in the seats and circus rings and hang the trapezes. I tell you, every man knew his job and it was interesting to watch. By ten o'clock in the morning everything was in order and ready for business. By noon the big circus parade would be on the street.

This was most interesting to me. We would spend the whole night watching the circus when it came to town. I would tell my young folk, "I'm of the opinion that this is the way it was done when the children of Israel came into camp."

When Israel came into camp, the Kohathites would put down the articles of furniture. Then Merari would come in with the boards and the bars and put up his part. Then Gershon would put on the coverings. Finally, the high priest would remove the veil and hang that. What a thrill it must have been to watch Israel come into camp. After forty years of practice they must have been pretty good at it.

As each Levite had his assignment, just so, every Christian has a gift and a job God wants him to do. I believe God will reward you for doing what He wants you to do. We are not to do what *we* choose to do, but we are to exercise the gifts that He has given us.

Suppose there was a fellow who carried that tent pin for the northwest corner of the tabernacle, and he got weary of his job. One day as he was driving in his pin, he said, "I'm tired of this. For twenty years now I've been carrying that tent pin. I come here in the morning, and loosen it and pull it out of the ground, put it on my shoulder, and take it over on the wagon with my family. Nobody seems to recognize how hard I work. Nobody rewards me for what I do. Moses never has called me up and given me a medal. I'm tired of this job and I'm going to quit carrying this pin." One morning when they were taking down the tabernacle, his pin was hard to loosen from the ground and he got disgusted and left it there. He thought, "Nobody will pay any attention anyway. My job is not very important. All I do is carry a tent pin; so I think I'll just leave it today."

Can you imagine the problem that next evening? They would try to set up the tabernacle, but the northwest corner pin would not be there. The men would report it to Moses, and they would look up this man who was to carry that pin. Moses would ask, "Where is the tent pin?" and the man would answer, "I left it back there where we camped last night." Then Moses would ask him why he left it, and the man would answer, "I don't think that my job is really important." Moses would say, "Not important! We can't put up the tabernacle without it. You will have to sit there all night holding that cord yourself because you are responsible for that tent pin!"

My friend, who is to determine who does the most important thing in God's service today? That man had been faithful for twenty years; then all of a sudden he just went haywire, and notice what it did to the setting up of the tabernacle. How many children of God today think their service is unimportant? God is not going to reward you for the amount of work you have done, but for your faithfulness in doing that which He has called you to do. If you are carrying that tent pin from the northwest corner, don't forget to carry it today. The job the Lord has given you to do is very important to Him.

CHAPTER 5

THEME: Defilement by disease and death; restitution;
the jealousy offering

You may have thought that Numbers is not a very interesting book,
but I hope that by now you have changed your mind. There is
interesting material in it and a pertinent message for us in these days.

We have seen the orderly arrangement of the camp which was a
preparation for the wilderness march. There had to be this preparation. The Christian today needs to recognize that he is a pilgrim going
through the wilderness of this world. Everything and everyone must
be in his place for the walk, the work, the war, and the worship of the
wilderness.

We come now to instructions concerning cleansing the camp,
which includes chapters 5 through 8. As we come to this section on
the cleansing of the camp, we need to recognize that the reason for
cleansing is that they (and we) are serving a holy God.

DEFILEMENT BY DISEASE AND DEATH

And the Lord spake unto Moses, saying,

Command the children of Israel, that they put out of the
camp every leper, and every one that hath an issue, and
whosoever is defiled by the dead:

Both male and female shall ye put out, without the
camp shall ye put them; that they defile not their camps,
in the midst whereof I dwell.

And the children of Israel did so, and put them out
without the camp: as the Lord spake unto Moses, so did
the children of Israel [Num. 5:1–4].

They were to put the leper out of the camp. That may seem cruel to us, but there was a very definite reason for it. There was the danger of contamination and transmission of disease. And we read that the camp was not to be defiled because God dwelt in the midst of the camp.

God commanded that certain ones were to be put out of the camp. This was not done by those who thought they were superior or wanted to assert their spiritual prerogatives. It was by *God's* command. Who were to be excluded from the camp? First of all, the leper. We saw in the Book of Leviticus that leprosy was a type of sin. Any outburst from within, an issue in the body, represents the flesh, the unregenerate nature of man. Sins of the flesh must be dealt with.

We need to recognize that if we are going to walk with God, if we are going to have fellowship with Him, there must be a cleansing of our lives. Recently I heard of a preacher who died as an alcoholic, yet people talked about what a blessing he was. I discount that, because God is not a fool. He does not bless nor will He walk with us when we are living in conscious sin. "For our God is a consuming fire" (Heb. 12:29). "God is greatly to be feared in the assembly of the saints, and to be had in reverence of all them that are about him" (Ps. 89:7). Today a great deal of the problems and difficulties and sickness and heartache is caused by Christian people who will not deal with the sin in their lives. In our churches today, we shut our eyes to sin in the lives of the people.

In Israel there were certain ones who had to be put out of the camp!

When we get to the Book of Joshua, we will see that Israel could not get a victory at Ai because Achan had sinned and had covered it up. It had to be brought to light and dealt with before Israel could have a victory.

I believe that there could be revival today if more preachers, church officers, Sunday school teachers, choir directors, and singers would deal with the sins in their lives. Sins of the flesh are like a leprosy. God will not bless until that sin is dealt with.

RESTITUTION

And the LORD spake unto Moses, saying,

Speak unto the children of Israel, When a man or woman shall commit any sin that men commit, to do a trespass against the LORD, and that person be guilty;

Then they shall confess their sin which they have done: and he shall recompense his trespass with the principal thereof, and add unto it the fifth part thereof, and give it unto him against whom he hath trespassed [Num. 5: 5–7].

This is what Zacchaeus was offering to do. "Behold, Lord, the half of my goods I give to the poor; and if I have taken any thing from any man by false accusation, I restore him fourfold" (Luke 19:8). He was actually going farther than the Mosaic Law required him to go.

We see here that a restitution was to be made. Repentance, therefore, is more than simply saying, "I'm sorry." A relationship between God and the individual cannot be made sweet until the relationship is made right between the individuals. "For godly sorrow worketh repentance to salvation not to be repented of: but the sorrow of the world worketh death" (2 Cor. 7:10). Many people today think that repentance means shedding a few tears and then going merrily on their way. It is much more than that. It is making things right by making restitution to the individual who has been injured. We are to confess our sins to God, that is true. But we must remember that our Lord also said this: "Therefore if thou bring thy gift to the altar, and there rememberest that thy brother hath ought against thee; Leave there thy gift before the altar, and go thy way; first be reconciled to thy brother, and then come and offer thy gift" (Matt. 5:23–24). The world has the idea one can shed a few tears and eat humble pie for a while and then everything is right again. That is what is called the "sorrow of the world" in Corinthians, and that kind of repentance is meaningless.

My Dad used to tell about a little boat on the Mississippi River. It had a little bitty boiler and a great big whistle. When that boat was going upstream and blew its whistle, it would drift back. It couldn't go upstream and blow its whistle at the same time! There are a lot of people like that today. Their repentance is like the blowing of the whistle. They shed tears in profusion, but there is no turning from sin, no turning to God, no restitution to the one they have injured. For this reason there is no progress in their Christian lives.

THE JEALOUSY OFFERING

And the Lord spake unto Moses, saying,

Speak unto the children of Israel, and say unto them, If any man's wife go aside, and commit a trespass against him,

And a man lie with her carnally, and it be hid from the eyes of her husband, and be kept close, and she be defiled, and there be no witness against her, neither she be taken with the manner;

And the spirit of jealousy come upon him, and he be jealous of his wife, and she be defiled: or if the spirit of jealousy come upon him, and he be jealous of his wife, and she be not defiled:

Then shall the man bring his wife unto the priest, and he shall bring her offering for her, the tenth part of an ephah of barley meal; he shall pour no oil upon it, nor put frankincense thereon; for it is an offering of jealousy, an offering of memorial, bringing iniquity to remembrance.

And the priest shall set the woman before the Lord, and uncover the woman's head, and put the offering of memorial in her hands, which is the jealousy offering: and the priest shall have in his hand the bitter water that causeth the curse:

And the priest shall charge her by an oath, and say unto the woman, If no man have lain with thee, and if thou hast not gone aside to uncleanness with another instead of thy husband, be thou free from this bitter water that causeth the curse [Num. 5:11–15, 18–19].

The verses following tell us that the woman was to drink the bitter water and if it caused her belly to swell and her thigh to rot, she was to be a curse among her people. If she was not defiled, but was clean, then she should be free. This test would have a tremendous psychological effect upon a person, especially if she were guilty.

Why isn't the man subjected to the same test? The Bible does not teach a double standard. In this case, the husband was suspicious of the wife. Could a husband be guilty? Of course. We saw in Leviticus, and will see again in Deuteronomy, that if a man or woman were taken in adultery, *both* of them were to be stoned to death. There is no double standard in the Bible. Then why is only the woman to be tested? Because this is a picture of Christ and the church. There can be no suspicion of Christ, but there is suspicion of the church, I can assure you. I know the church rather well, and, believe me, it is under suspicion!

But this is a jealousy offering. Can God be jealous? Yes, He says that He is a jealous God. Many times He says, "I the LORD thy God am a jealous God." It is not the low human kind of jealousy like the jealousy of a person who is goaded by an Iago, but the jealousy of love.

When I hear a wife say, "My husband is not jealous of me," I want to say to her, "Lady, don't mention it. If your husband is not jealous of you, it is because he doesn't love you. So I don't think I would mention it, if I were you." If a man really loves a woman, he is jealous of her, and the same thing would be true of a woman who loves a man. This is the way God is jealous. He loves us, and He wants our love in return. He is jealous of us! He doesn't want us to give our time and our affection to the things of this world.

Now, in this test of jealousy, if the wife was shown to be innocent, she was exonerated. Actually, this law protected her from a jealous husband. This worked in her behalf in a very wonderful way.

Certainly this reveals again that the Word of God is very clear on this matter of fidelity to the marriage vow. Today we are seeing a great letdown of that, and it is becoming the accepted thing that the marriage vow is not to be taken seriously. God will hold you to it—I can assure you of that. A great many of the problems of this world today begin in the home. They are being made by those who are treating lightly the marriage vow. God cannot, nor will He bless a nation where this situation prevails.

CHAPTER 6

THEME: Nazarite vow; the triune blessing

We come now to something that is quite remarkable: the vow of the Nazarite. This was a voluntary vow. Any man or woman of Israel who wanted to become a Nazarite could do so. He could take the vow for a certain period of time or for a lifetime. God did not command it; it was purely voluntary. But if any of His people wanted a closer walk with Him, this is what they could do.

NAZARITE VOW

And the LORD spake unto Moses, saying,

Speak unto the children of Israel, and say unto them, When either man or woman shall separate themselves to vow a vow of a Nazarite, to separate themselves unto the LORD:

He shall separate himself from wine and strong drink, and shall drink no vinegar of wine, or vinegar of strong drink, neither shall he drink any liquor of grapes, nor eat moist grapes, or dried [Num. 6:1–3].

When a person took this voluntary vow of the Nazarite, there were three things he was forbidden to do.

First, he was not to drink wine or strong drink. Anything that came from the vine was forbidden him. This has nothing to do with the question of whether it is right or wrong to drink wine. May I say this, and I want to say it carefully and I want you to hear me carefully. The Christian standard is not a standard of right or wrong. The question is this: What is your *purpose* in doing what you are doing? Are you doing it to please Christ? Do you want to be a Nazarite? Do you want to live for Him? That is the question. People will ask me whether it is right for a Christian to drink wine. My friend, I won't argue that point. I won't argue right or wrong with you. I want to know whether you really want to please Christ. Wine, in the Scriptures, is a symbol of earthly joy; it is to cheer the heart. The whole point here is that the Nazarite was to find his joy in the Lord.

There are a great many Christians today who do not find their joy in the things of God, in the Word of God, or in fellowship with Christ. They find their joy in the things of this world. I go to a great number of church banquets, and I know there are church members there who would never come to a weekday meeting unless it was a banquet. I always feel sorry for those Christians who, like the poor woman, got crumbs from God's table. Don't misunderstand me; there is nothing wrong with banquets, but when they go to Christian banquets, they get crumbs—that's all. There would be the time of eating, then a few pious things would be said; someone would take a verse of Scripture and say some sweet things about it, and everyone would leave, feeling very spiritual and very satisfied and even challenged. But they would drop right back and live just as they had always lived. I feel sorry for them.

Where do you find joy, friend? I ask you that very personally. Do you need the stimulants of this world in order to enjoy "Christian" things? Can you really get joy out of studying the Word of God? Does prayer turn you off or turn you on? My, how many of us today think we are being really Christian and really spiritual when all we have been doing is bringing the world into our activities!

Second, when a person took the Nazarite vow, he was not to shave his head.

> **All the days of the vow of his separation there shall no razor come upon his head: until the days be fulfilled, in the which he separateth himself unto the LORD, he shall be holy, and shall let the locks of the hair of his head grow [Num. 6:5].**

Paul says in 1 Corinthians 11:14, "Doth not even nature itself teach you, that, if a man have long hair, it is a shame unto him?" I wish we could hang signs to state this in public places. I still think it is a shame for a man to have long hair. I agree with the apostle Paul; it is a shame to the man. Therefore, the Nazarite must be willing to bear shame for Christ. His long hair would indicate that he was willing to share that position with Christ who said, "But I am a worm, and no man; a reproach of men, and despised of the people" (Ps. 22:6).

Third, he who took the Nazarite vow was not to touch a dead body.

> **All the days that he separateth himself unto the LORD he shall come at no dead body.**
>
> **He shall not make himself unclean for his father, or for his mother, for his brother, or for his sister, when they die: because the consecration of his God is upon his head [Num. 6:6–7].**

We read in chapter 5 that a leper was to be taken out of the camp and also whoever was defiled by the dead. You see, the world is the place of death. I think one can say that death is the deepest mark that is on this world today. Death is the seal of a sin-cursed earth. It is the judgment which God pronounced. It was because of sin that death came into the world. In order to deal with death, sin must be dealt with, because the wages of sin is death.

The Nazarite was not to touch a dead body. He was to be separate from the world. The Lord was to be first in his life. Remember the Lord Jesus said, "He that loveth father or mother more than me is not worthy of me: and he that loveth son or daughter more than me is not worthy of me" (Matt. 10:37). He is to be put above loved ones. He has top priority. Remember that this vow is voluntary. He doesn't command the vow of the Nazarite. But if one wanted to take this vow and dedicate his life to Him, he could do so.

Do you find your joy in the Lord? Are you willing to bear shame for Him, to take a humble place for Him? Are you willing to put Him first, above everything in this life? You see, although the believer today doesn't take a Nazarite vow, there is the offer of a closer walk with the Lord. It is voluntary. You must want it. It is an act of dedication. It is incorrect to call it consecration; you cannot consecrate yourself. Only God can consecrate you. Actually, what we do is come to God with empty hands, offering nothing but ourselves to Him—our devotion, our worship, our love, our service, our time.

Sometimes when you stand for God, you will find you must stand alone. He must be first in your life. Many people today talk about being consecrated Christians, but they wouldn't dare do anything that would offend the little clique in their church. They are afraid they might find themselves outside, which would be much better for them because some of these church cliques are not of God and can be a very cruel crowd! Yet, there are folk who think they are consecrated, who do not have the strength or stamina to stand against such a clique; so they just go along with the crowd. You see, if you want to give yourself to the Lord, Christ must have top priority. You must find your satisfaction and your joy in Him.

All the days of his separation he is holy unto the Lord [Num. 6:8].

I'm of the opinion that a great many folk today are missing a great blessing. Perhaps even now you are going through a particular time of trial. Why not set yourself aside for God? If you are a Christian, give yourself to God in a very definite way. It won't remove the trial, but it will make it more bearable. The Lord Jesus said, "Come unto me, all ye that labour and are heavy laden, and I will give you rest. Take my yoke upon you, and learn of me; for I am meek and lowly in heart: and ye shall find rest unto your souls" (Matt. 11:28–29). It is wonderful to be yoked with Him.

And if any man die very suddenly by him, and he hath defiled the head of his consecration; then he shall shave his head in the day of his cleansing, on the seventh day shall he shave it.

> And on the eighth day he shall bring two turtles, or two young pigeons, to the priest, to the door of the tabernacle of the congregation [Num. 6:9–10].

God is very earnest about having a vow to Him kept. If the Nazarite was defiled, he was to bring a sacrifice. God does not require a vow, but when a vow is made, He expects it to be kept, and it is a serious matter if it is broken.

I am confident that there are a great many Christians who promised God things that they never made good, and that explains their sad spiritual plight today. Through the years of my ministry, I have watched some people come to church every Sunday with their halos brightly shined. They would be so pious that you'd think any moment they would sprout wings and fly away. Yet, these people would let the Lord down, over and over again. Then, later on, something would come up in their lives that would make shipwreck of their faith.

A great many people today will not make a pledge to God because they are afraid they may not keep it. People are afraid to put it on the line with God. They are afraid to pledge something financial, for example, because they might see a new car or a new television set and buy that instead. So they don't want to commit themselves about something to God. May I say, I believe this is one reason people miss out on blessings today.

Now it is true, God goes into great detail here to reveal that He does expect us to follow through right down to the details. It is also true that we shouldn't pledge something to God and then decide to do something or to buy something else instead. But, if we make an agreement with God and stick with it, He will bless. God is very serious and very practical about these matters, and we should be also. God will always bless us if we are faithful to Him and to the promise we make to Him. There is a great spiritual lesson here for us. This is something you should think about very seriously today.

THE TRIUNE BLESSING

And the LORD spake unto Moses, saying,

Speak unto Aaron and unto his sons, saying, On this
wise ye shall bless the children of Israel, saying unto
them,

The LORD bless thee, and keep thee:

The LORD make his face shine upon thee, and be gracious unto thee:

The LORD lift up his countenance upon thee, and give
thee peace.

And they shall put my name upon the children of Israel;
and I will bless them [Num. 6:22–27].

Here we find the Trinity in the Old Testament. God the Father is the
source of all blessing. The Lord Jesus is the One who makes His face to
shine upon us. The Holy Spirit lifts up His countenance upon us and
gives us peace. This is the only way we can come to God and experience the peace of God. He is the One who makes these things real to
our hearts.

The triune God gives them this blessing. The census has been
taken, and they all know their pedigree. The standards have been
raised; so they all know where they belong. They are to follow their
standard, and they are to camp in their assigned place in the camp
with their own tribe and their own family. The camp has been
cleansed. Now the Lord blesses them. It is the only way God can bless.

Many churches today are not experiencing the blessing of God.
The problem is that they are not properly prepared for the march.
They are trying to start out without first setting things in order. They
are like a soldier who forgot to put on his belt one morning. Believe
me it is pretty hard to march and carry a gun without your belt or
suspenders! And there are churches like that, my friend. They are
starting out before things are set in order. Paul is writing to the church
when he says, "Let all things be done decently and in order" (1 Cor.
14:40). Know your pedigree; that is, know you are a child of God;

know your standard; know what your gift is and use it for Him; and keep your life clean.

What a wonderful blessing there is here. God the Father keeps us; the Son makes His face to shine upon us—He is the light of the world; God the Holy Spirit gives us peace. What a glorious chapter this is!

CHAPTER 7

THEME: Gifts of the princes

We come now to another rather remarkable chapter. This is next to the longest chapter in the Bible. The longest chapter in the Bible is Psalm 119, which is all about the Word of God. Here we find eighty-nine verses, and do you know what they are all about? The gifts of the princes. They enumerate each item that they brought. It's really a monotonous chapter, because it is repetition again and again. All the princes are mentioned, and we are told exactly what each one of them gave. This has a very important message for you and me.

GIFTS OF THE PRINCES

And it came to pass on the day that Moses had fully set up the tabernacle, and had anointed it, and sanctified it, and all the instruments thereof, both the altar and all the vessels thereof, and had anointed them, and sanctified them;

That the princes of Israel, heads of the house of their fathers, who were the princes of the tribes, and were over them that were numbered, offered:

And the LORD said unto Moses, They shall offer their offering, each prince on his day, for the dedicating of the altar.

And he that offered his offering the first day was Nahshon the son of Amminadab, of the tribe of Judah:

And his offering was one silver charger, the weight thereof was an hundred and thirty shekels, one silver bowl of seventy shekels, after the shekel of the sanctuary; both of them were full of fine flour mingled with oil for a meat offering:

One spoon of ten shekels of gold, full of incense:

One young bullock, one ram, one lamb of the first year, for a burnt offering:

One kid of the goats for a sin offering:

And for a sacrifice of peace offerings, two oxen, five rams, five he goats, five lambs of the first year: this was the offering of Nahshon the son of Amminadab [Num. 7:1-2, 11-17].

Do you know this man, Nahshon? I don't. All I know about this man is that he offered these gifts, but God knew him and God took note of the gifts that he brought.

Do you find his offering interesting? I don't, really. It sounds sort of like a shopping list.

Now the next man came:

On the second day Nethaneel the son of Zuar, prince of Issachar, did offer [Num. 7:18].

Now do you know what he did? He did the same thing—brought the identical offering. Couldn't the Bible just have a ditto mark there for his offering? Couldn't the Spirit of God have said simply that it was the same? No, the Spirit of God recorded very carefully and in detail what each one brought. Each man is listed here by name, and as far as I know, this is all he ever did for the Lord. This whole long chapter is about these men and what they gave to the Lord. Even a spoonful of incense was recorded!

Now, our Lord said, "But when thou doest alms, let not thy left hand know what thy right hand doeth" (Matt. 6:3), and a great many people had better not let the right hand know what the left hand is doing, because both hands are doing so little for the Lord. They should be ashamed of their hands, both right and left. But I have news for you. Little as it is, the Lord records what you do for Him.

Remember that the Gospel of Luke tells how the Lord Jesus sat over against the treasury one day. Was He nosy, do you think? Did He have any business there? He certainly did. He just happened to be the Lord of Glory and the Lord of the temple. He watched how the people gave. The rich gave rich gifts. They were large gifts, and He noted that. Then He watched a widow put in two little coppers. In comparison to the richness of that temple, to the ornateness and wealth of it, she didn't add anything. But Jesus didn't think of it that way. She gave all she had, and to Jesus hers was the largest gift of all. It is recorded in heaven. You may be sure of that.

Jesus knows exactly what you give to Him, and He knows how much you keep for yourself. I don't like this pious talk of some people saying what they give is just between them and the Lord. I wonder if they realize the Lord is recording it.

The tabernacle erected, and the tents of Israel around it.

This is a remarkable chapter. It is eighty-nine verses long, and one of the most monotonous things I've ever read, but I think the Lord still looks it over. I think He opens the books and says, "Well, look here what this prince gave." He takes note of all the gifts.

Friend, you have never done anything for Him that is not recorded, and you will be rewarded for that. We ought to talk more freely about these things because they are important to God.

CHAPTER 8

THEME: The light of the lampstand; Levites cleansed

This chapter surprises us by beginning with instructions for lighting the lampstand in the Holy Place. At first it seems that the lampstand is out of place—that it belongs back in Exodus where instructions were given for the tabernacle. But as we look at it more closely, we see that God has a good reason for mentioning it here.

Chapter 8 continues the section regarding the cleansing operation in preparation for the wilderness march. Those who were going to follow God and serve Him had to be clean.

THE LIGHT OF THE LAMPSTAND

And the LORD spake unto Moses, saying,

Speak unto Aaron, and say unto him, When thou lightest the lamps, the seven lamps shall give light over against the candlestick.

And Aaron did so; he lighted the lamps thereof over against the candlestick, as the LORD commanded Moses.

And this work of the candlestick was of beaten gold, unto the shaft thereof, unto the flowers thereof, was beaten work: according unto the pattern which the LORD had shewed Moses, so he made the candlestick [Num. 8:1–4].

This beautiful lampstand was one of the articles of furniture in the tabernacle. It was made of beaten gold, the work of an artisan who had shaped it into the form of branches of almonds with a great almond blossom at the top of each branch to hold the lamps. The lights on the top revealed the beauty of the lampstand.

This is the most perfect picture of Christ that we find in the tabernacle. The lighted lamps represent the Holy Spirit who reveals the beauty of Christ. The lampstand is symbolic of Christ who sent the Holy Spirit into the world. The Spirit of God takes the things of Christ and shows them to us.

Now we understand why the lampstand is mentioned here between the gifts of the princes and the cleansing of the Levites. It reminds us that everything must be done in the light of the presence of Christ.

What does that mean to you and me? It means that our gifts to Him and our service for Him must be done in the light of His presence. In other words, it must be done according to His Word. This is where the church is to get its instructions—not from a book of church order or some other place—but from the Word of God.

The lampstand is the light, and the Lord Jesus Christ calls Himself the Light of the world. He is revealed in the Word of God.

LEVITES CLEANSED

The remainder of the chapter deals with the cleansing of the Levites. They had to come to the laver for cleansing although they had already been to the brazen altar, which speaks of the Cross of Christ. Now we find that God will keep His servants clean.

And the LORD spake unto Moses, saying,

Take the Levites from among the children of Israel, and cleanse them [Num. 8:5-6].

Friend, if God is going to use you, He'll have to clean you. He will have His own way of doing it. Now notice how the Levites were cleansed.

And thus shalt thou do unto them, to cleanse them: Sprinkle water of purifying upon them, and let them shave all their flesh, and let them wash their clothes, and so make themselves clean.

Then let them take a young bullock with his meat offering, even fine flour mingled with oil, and another young bullock shalt thou take for a sin offering [Num. 8:7-8].

First, they must be sprinkled with the water of purifying. This was done at the laver. Secondly, they were to shave all their flesh. Thirdly, they were to wash their clothes to make themselves clean. Fourthly, they were to offer a sin offering and a burnt offering.

Do you remember what God has said about Levi? Levi was one of the sons of Jacob, and when Jacob blessed him, this is what he said: "Simeon and Levi are brethren; instruments of cruelty are in their habitations. O my soul, come not thou into their secret; unto their assembly, mine honour, be not thou united: for in their anger they slew a man, and in their selfwill they digged down a wall. Cursed be their anger, for it was fierce; and their wrath, for it was cruel: I will divide them in Jacob, and scatter them in Israel" (Gen. 49:5-7). Obviously they needed to be cleansed.

The important thing for the child of God today is not *how* you walk, but *where* you walk. "But if we walk in the light, as he is in the light, we have fellowship one with another, and the blood of Jesus Christ his Son cleanseth us from all sin" (1 John 1:7). You see, the light and the laver are placed together here. When you walk in the light, you see that there is imperfection in your life. Then you go to the laver to remove it, which symbolizes the confession of your sins.

Notice that there are four steps that are given here for cleansing.

1. "Sprinkle water of purifying upon them." You remember that when Christ washed the disciples' feet, Simon Peter objected. The Lord Jesus told him, "If I wash thee not, thou hast no part with me" (John 13:8). That means, you will not have fellowship with Me, you will have no part with Me. John explains this in his Epistle. "But if we walk in the light, as he is in the light, we have fellowship one with another." Yes, but when I walk in the light, I see things that are

wrong in my life. What am I to do then? "And the blood of Jesus Christ his Son cleanseth us from all sin." It keeps on cleansing us from all sin as we confess our sins to Him. "If we confess our sins, he is faithful and just to forgive us our sins, and to cleanse us from all unrighteousness" (1 John 1:7 and 9). This is most important, friends. This is for believers. If you are to serve God, you must confess your sins. The brazen altar is the place where the sinner comes to God for salvation; the laver is the place the believer, the saint of God, comes to be cleansed.

2. "Let them shave all their flesh." The word of God is alive, and "powerful, and sharper than any two-edged sword, piercing even to the dividing asunder of soul and spirit, and of the joints and marrow, and is a discerner of the thoughts and intents of the heart" (Heb. 4:12). The Word of God can dig down into your life and find things wrong there that you didn't know were wrong. You don't need that sharp razor, you see. You don't think there is a spot on you? Then get out the razor and start using the Word of God. It's a light and it's also a sharp razor.

3. "Let them wash their clothes." A garment speaks of the habits of life. We even call them a riding habit or a walking habit to identify the use of the garment. We need to wash our garments—we have certain habits that we need to get rid of because they are hurting our testimony for the Lord.

4. "Take for a sin offering." There was to be a bullock for a burnt offering and a meal offering and another young bullock for a sin offering. These offerings, as we have already seen, speak of Christ. The burnt offering speaks of who He is. The meal offering speaks of His sinless perfection. The peace offering speaks of the fact that He made peace by the blood of His Cross. The sin offering speaks of what He has done for us. In other words, all of this cleansing, all of this that is done, is done in the light of the person and work of Christ. He did all of this for us. He did it in order that we might serve Him.

> And thou shalt bring the Levites before the tabernacle of the congregation: and thou shalt gather the whole assembly of the children of Israel together:

> And thou shalt bring the Levites before the LORD: and the
> children of Israel shall put their hands upon the Levites:
>
> And Aaron shall offer the Levites before the LORD for an
> offering of the children of Israel, that they may execute
> the service of the LORD [Num. 8:9–11].

Now, let us understand this very clearly. You can sing a solo, you can
preach a sermon, you can teach a Sunday school class, you can be an
officer in the church, but you are not effective until you walk in the
light of the Word of God, until you have been to Him for cleansing.
You must see yourself in the light of the Word of God. You know you
come short, you confess your sins to Him, and you know He forgives
you and cleanses you. You use that sharp razor that takes off that
which offends. You need to watch your habits if you are to be used of
God. Many a man has let a bad habit ruin his testimony. And the
cleansing must all rest upon the person and work of Christ.

We see that all this was done so that the Levites might serve the
Lord.

> Thus shalt thou separate the Levites from among the
> children of Israel: and the Levites shall be mine.
>
> And I have given the Levites as a gift to Aaron and to his
> sons from among the children of Israel, to do the service
> of the children of Israel in the tabernacle of the congre-
> gation, and to make an atonement for the children of Is-
> rael: that there be no plague among the children of
> Israel, when the children of Israel come nigh unto the
> sanctuary [Num. 8:14, 19].

Remember that we have mentioned before how our Lord, in His high
priestly prayer, says of the believers, ". . . thine they were, and thou
gavest them me . . ." (John 17:6). The Lord Jesus Christ paid a price
and redeemed us back to God by His own blood. Now the Father has
given us a gift back to the Lord Jesus Christ. We belong to Him.

Now service to Him does not rest upon rules and regulations and law. That is not the way to serve the Lord Jesus. We serve Him because we love Him. We are in a new relationship to Him. We have been joined to Him; we are a part of Him. What a thrill it is to know it is not a matter of following little rules and regulations. Instead it is a matter of wanting to please Him. How wonderful this is.

> **This is it that belongeth unto the Levites: from twenty and five years old and upward they shall go in to wait upon the service of the tabernacle of the congregation:**
>
> **And from the age of fifty years they shall cease waiting upon the service thereof, and shall serve no more:**
>
> **But shall minister with their brethren in the tabernacle of the congregation, to keep the charge, and shall do no service. Thus shalt thou do unto the Levites touching their charge [Num. 8:24–26].**

The Levites were permitted to serve in the tabernacle at the age of twenty-five years. Back in the fourth chapter we learned that they could not enter into priestly service until the age of thirty years. The priests served from age thirty to fifty. The Levites who served around in the tabernacle, putting it up, taking it down—just any kind of service—were from age twenty-five to fifty years. Back in Numbers 1:3 we saw that the census of those able to go to war included the ones who were twenty years old and upward.

This raises the question of the age of accountability. When we come to Numbers 14:29 we read, "Your carcases shall fall in this wilderness; and all that were numbered of you, according to your whole number, from twenty years old and upward, which have murmured against me." Apparently in this instance, twenty years was the age of accountability. The boy who was nineteen years old would be permitted to enter the land. The twenty-year-old boy who had murmured would die in the wilderness.

I would like to suggest that the age of accountability may be older than we tend to think it is. We think maybe a little child is responsible. I don't think so. A little child can accept the Lord. In fact there are many on record as young as four years old who have received Christ. But the age of accountability must be somewhat later than that, and I'm of the opinion it will be different for different people. We see here that God made it different for the different forms of service. A man could be a soldier at twenty years; a Levite could work in the tabernacle at twenty-five years; a priest began his priestly service at thirty years. The important thing is that we should instruct boys and girls and encourage them to come to the Lord as soon as possible. It is so important for our children to trust in the Lord Jesus.

CHAPTER 9

THEME: Passover observed on wilderness march; pillar of cloud by day, pillar of fire by night.

PASSOVER OBSERVED ON WILDERNESS MARCH

And the Lord spake unto Moses in the wilderness of Sinai, in the first month of the second year after they were come out of the land of Egypt, saying,

Let the children of Israel also keep the passover at his appointed season [Num. 9:1–2].

Israel was to celebrate the Passover while they were in the wilderness. So they kept the Passover on this, the second year after they left Egypt. During the celebration a problem arose. There were certain men who were defiled by a dead body so that they could not keep the Passover. They came and reported it to Moses and Aaron and asked what they should do.

And Moses said unto them, Stand still, and I will hear what the Lord will command concerning you [Num. 9:8].

Moses didn't appeal to a book of church order; he didn't appeal to *Robert's Rules of Order*. He appealed to God. I repeat again what I have said so often. We are to appeal to the Word of God today. That is the authority for the child of God. Now I realize there will be different ideas on the interpretation of the Word of God. That is why we should study it and be sensible in our interpretation of it.

And the Lord spake unto Moses, saying,

Speak unto the children of Israel, saying, If any man of you or of your posterity shall be unclean by reason of a

> dead body, or be in a journey afar off, yet he shall keep
> the passover unto the LORD.

> The fourteenth day of the second month at even they
> shall keep it, and eat it with unleavened bread and bitter
> herbs [Num. 9:9–11].

Those who were unable to keep the Passover at the appointed time
were to have a delayed Passover and celebrate it a month later.

PILLAR OF CLOUD BY DAY, PILLAR OF FIRE BY NIGHT

> And on the day that the tabernacle was reared up the
> cloud covered the tabernacle, namely, the tent of the tes-
> timony: and at even there was upon the tabernacle as it
> were the appearance of fire, until the morning.

> So it was alway: the cloud covered it by day, and the ap-
> pearance of fire by night [Num. 9:15–16].

The children of Israel had a covering cloud, which was the Skekinah
glory. This was one of many things that made them different from any
other nation. When Paul was writing to the Romans and wanted to
give some of the identifying marks of the Israelites, he wrote this,
"Who are Israelites; to whom pertaineth the adoption, and the glory,
and the covenants, and the giving of the law, and the service of God,
and the promises; Whose are the fathers, and of whom as concerning
the flesh Christ came, who is over all, God blessed for ever. Amen"
(Rom. 9:4–5). You see, he mentions the glory. These were the only
people who ever had the visible presence of God with them.

> At the commandment of the LORD the children of Israel
> journeyed, and at the commandment of the LORD they
> pitched: as long as the cloud abode upon the tabernacle
> they rested in their tents.

> And when the cloud tarried long upon the tabernacle
> many days, then the children of Israel kept the charge of
> the LORD, and journeyed not [Num. 9:18-19].

Moses was not the only one who decided whether they would march today or tomorrow, or whether they would stay in camp for several days. God decided that.

We need to recognize today that the Lord Jesus Christ is the Head of the church. He is the One who should lead. The problem is that the church is so busy going its own way that oftentimes He isn't even consulted. But Christ is still the Head of His church, and those who are His will follow Him.

You will notice that sometimes they stayed in camp for several days, even months, and they were about a year at Mount Sinai. They were out there in that wilderness for forty years.

> Or whether it were two days, or a month, or a year, that
> the cloud tarried upon the tabernacle, remaining
> thereon, the children of Israel abode in their tents, and
> journeyed not: but when it was taken up, they jour-
> neyed.
>
> At the commandment of the LORD they rested in the
> tents, and at the commandment of the LORD they jour-
> neyed: they kept the charge of the LORD, at the com-
> mandment of the LORD by the hand of Moses [Num.
> 9:22-23].

When the pillar of cloud lifted in the morning, they knew it was a day for them to journey. The Levites would go immediately to take down the tabernacle, and I believe they could do this in thirty minutes or so, and would put it up just as quickly in the evening when they came to rest. Then the pillar of cloud that had led them would settle down over the tabernacle. This pillar of cloud and pillar of fire was the Ske-kinah glory that was the visible presence of God. After their wilderness journey was over, and they were settled in the land, Solomon erected a temple to replace the mobile tabernacle. "And it came to pass, when the priests were come out of the holy place, that the cloud filled the house of the LORD, So that the priests could not stand to minister because of the cloud: for the glory of the LORD had filled the house of the LORD" (1 Kings 8:10–11). God, you see, hallowed the temple with His presence. However, later in their history when Israel turned from her God, the Shekinah glory left the temple. Ezekiel tells of its hesitant departure, as though reluctant to leave, then of its lifting up and disappearance into the heavens.

Of the Lord Jesus, John wrote, "And we beheld his glory," but not many saw it at His first coming. It was His glory that He laid aside when He came to this earth—not His deity, but His glory.

When He comes again, there will be "the sign of the Son of man in heaven," and I believe that sign will be the Shekinah glory. Christ will return to earth in all His glory.

That sign is not for the church. We are never given a visible presence of God. Rather, we are given the *inward* presence of God, the Holy Spirit indwelling us. The Spirit of God is *in* the believer today. What wonderful truths there are here for us.

CHAPTER 10

THEME: Silver trumpets; order of march

The last preparation for the march is the instructions for making two silver trumpets. The wilderness march will then begin in verse 11 of this chapter.

SILVER TRUMPETS

And the LORD spake unto Moses, saying,

Make thee two trumpets of silver; of a whole piece shalt thou make them: that thou mayest use them for the calling of the assembly, and for the journeying of the camps [Num. 10:1–2].

Two is the number of witnesses—it is in the mouth of two witnesses that a matter is established. These two trumpets were used to move Israel on the wilderness march.

And when they shall blow with them, all the assembly shall assemble themselves to thee at the door of the tabernacle of the congregation.

And if they blow but with one trumpet, then the princes, which are heads of the thousands of Israel, shall gather themselves unto thee [Num. 10:3–4].

The blowing of one trumpet brought the princes together. This reminds us that there is to be a last trump for the church. That last trump, I believe, is the voice of Christ which will be His last call. He has sent out invitation after invitation. His final invitation to the Laodicean church is "Behold, I stand at the door, and knock: if any man hear my voice, and open the door, I will come in to him, and will sup with him, and he with me" (Rev. 3:20). At the last trump, He will call His church out of the world. That will be the last call. The one single trumpet, which is the voice of the Lord Jesus, will bring the believers together. This is what we call the Rapture of the church.

> When ye blow an alarm, then the camps that lie on the east parts shall go forward.
>
> When ye blow an alarm the second time, then the camps that lie on the south side shall take their journey: they shall blow an alarm for their journeys.
>
> But when the congregation is to be gathered together, ye shall blow, but ye shall not sound an alarm [Num. 10:5-7].

The trumpets were used to bring this tremendous number of people into formation for the march through the wilderness.

> And if ye go to war in your land against the enemy that oppresseth you, then ye shall blow an alarm with the trumpets; and ye shall be remembered before the LORD your God, and ye shall be saved from your enemies [Num. 10:9].

Another use of the trumpets was to blow the alarm for war.

> Also in the day of your gladness, and in your solemn days, and in the beginnings of your months, ye shall blow with the trumpets over your burnt offerings, and over the sacrifices of your peace offerings; that they may be to you for a memorial before your God: I am the LORD your God [Num. 10:10].

The sounding of the trumpets also would denote certain segments of time and special occasions.

These trumpets, made of silver, which is the metal of redemption, sounded the call for a redeemed people. This was the way God moved them on the wilderness march. They were used as a way of signalling to the people how they should march through the wilderness.

ORDER OF MARCH

And it came to pass on the twentieth day of the second month, in the second year, that the cloud was taken up from off the tabernacle of the testimony.

And the children of Israel took their journeys out of the wilderness of Sinai; and the cloud rested in the wilderness of Paran [Num. 10:11–12].

They have been here at Sinai for about a year, getting the Law from God. The instructions for the silver trumpets have been given, and the trumpets have been made. Now they are blown and the children of Israel begin their wilderness march.

This becomes very detailed in its instructions here in this chapter. Let us go back for a moment to the plan of encampment which we had in chapter 2. You remember that the families of Levi were encamped around the tabernacle. Moses and Aaron were on the east side, Merari on the north, Gershon on the west, and Kohath on the south. Then the camps of the twelve tribes were out beyond that. Judah, Issachar, and Zebulun were on the east; Dan, Ashur, and Naphtali on the north; Ephraim, Manasseh, and Benjamin on the west; and Reuben, Simeon, and Gad on the south.

Early one morning the people of Israel strike camp because the

THE ORDER BY WHICH THEY MARCHED IS GIVEN IN 10:11–36:

Mixed Multitude	*Section 7* Dan *bearing standard* (vs. 25)	*Section 6* Ephraim *bearing standard* (vs. 22)	*Section 5* Kohathites *bearing sanctuary* (vs. 21)	*Section 4* Reuben *bearing standard* (vs. 18)
	Asher Naphtali	Manasseh Benjamin	Sons of Levi	Simeon Gad

pillar of cloud is lifted. Each family packs their things; the tabernacle is taken down. The time has come to move. What do they do first? Moses and Aaron give the signal and the silver trumpets are blown to sound an alarm. Who moves first? The family of Kohath which carries the ark moves out in front. The ark leads the wilderness march.

Also Christ leads His church through the wilderness of this world. The ark is a picture of Jesus Christ.

So the first trumpet puts Moses and Aaron and the ark out in front. The trumpet blows again and Judah moves out from the east side, with Issachar and Zebulun marching with Judah under his banner. After them come Gershon and Merari, bearing their part of the tabernacle—they had the heavier things, such as the boards and the bars and the coverings. Then the trumpet blows and Reuben with Simeon and Gad move out, marching under the standard of Reuben. The trumpet blows again and the Kohathites follow them. They are carrying all the articles of furniture of the tabernacle except the ark, which has gone ahead to the front of the march. All these articles of furniture were equipped with poles and the Kohathites bore them on their shoulders. The trumpet sounds again and Ephraim moves out with Manasseh and Benjamin under his standard. Finally, Dan moves out with Asher and Naphtali, under the standard of Dan. Bringing up the rear is the mixed multitude, folk who were part Israelite and part Egyptian. They didn't know whether they should stay or go. Each one was mixed up. As a result, they were stragglers who came along on the wilderness march. The young man who blasphemed (whom we read about in Leviticus 24), who had an Egyptian father and an Israelite mother, had been part of this group.

Did you notice that the trumpet was blown seven times? In the Book of Revelation there is the blowing of the seven trumpets. Those

Section 3	Section 2	Section 1		
Gershon	Judah	Moses		
Merari	"Praise"	Aaron	Ark	
bearing tabernacle	*bearing standard*			
(vs. 17)	(vs. 14)	(vs. 33)		
				FORWARD
Sons of Levi	Issachar			MARCH
	Zebulun			

seven trumpets are connected with the children of Israel. The blowing of those trumpets in the Great Tribulation period will move the children of Israel from all corners of the earth back into that land.

A great many people try to associate the last trump that is mentioned in 1 Corinthians 15:52 with the last trumpet in the Book of Revelation, and then they draw the conclusion that the church is going through the Great Tribulation period. However, that last trump which is mentioned in Corinthians is the voice of the Son of God, which is detailed in 1 Thessalonians 4:16, "For the Lord himself shall descend from heaven with a shout, with the voice of the archangel, and with the trump of God. . . ." His voice is like the voice of an archangel and like the sound of a trumpet. We know this because in Revelation 1:10–11 John writes, "I was in the Spirit on the Lord's day, and heard behind me a great voice, as of a trumpet, Saying, I am Alpha and Omega, the first and the last. . . ." Whom did John see when he turned to see who had spoken to him? He saw the glorified Christ, the Great High Priest. *His* voice is like a trumpet. His voice is going to raise the dead and change the mortal bodies of those who are living when He comes for His church. The trumpet sound for the church is the voice of the Son of God.

Trumpets are connected with the children of Israel. It is the trumpet that moved them on the wilderness march. It will be the trumpets that will bring them from the wilderness of this world back into the land.

> **And Moses said unto Hobab, the son of Raguel the Midianite, Moses' father in law, We are journeying unto the place of which the LORD said, I will give it to you: come thou with us, and we will do thee good: for the LORD hath spoken good concerning Israel [Num. 10:29].**

Here we have recorded an encounter with Moses' father-in-law and Moses' invitation to him. This could be applied to the church. We are strangers and pilgrims going through this world today. We are in a wilderness here, but we are on the way to the presence of the Lord

Jesus Christ. Our invitation is the same invitation that Moses gave, "Come thou with us."

If you are not a child of God by faith in Jesus Christ, you may join the party. It is a great one, by the way, as we are marching to go into the presence of Jesus Christ. We are not a group that is marching because we are better than anyone else. We are sinners who have been saved by the grace of God. If you see yourself as a sinner and you need a Savior, turn to Him by simple faith and trust Him. Join the march! This is no protest march; it is a salvation march, a redemption march. It is the march that is going to Zion, not the earthly Zion but the heavenly one, the city of Jerusalem which will come down from God out of heaven, adorned like a bride for the bridegroom.

> **And he said unto him, I will not go; but I will depart to mine own land, and to my kindred [Num. 10:30].**

Now Moses keeps on talking, and maybe he shouldn't have done that. Old Hobab, the father-in-law, didn't want to go along. He wanted to go home. So Moses answered him,

> **And he said, Leave us not, I pray thee; forasmuch as thou knowest how we are to encamp in the wilderness, and thou mayest be to us instead of eyes [Num. 10:31].**

I want to say to you right here that I don't understand Moses. God has made it clear to Moses that the pillar of cloud by day and the pillar of fire by night would guide them and that the ark was leading them, both of which speak of Christ. He is the leader. Now Moses is suggesting to his own father-in-law that he needs him to lead them. The old man had been raised in the desert in Midian. He was a Midianite and he knew that area. He could have been a great help, I'm sure. But, you see, they were not to depend upon natural means. This old man didn't know the way God wanted them to go.

Unfortunately, the church is listening to the voice of the "experts," men without real spiritual discernment. As a result, the church is be-

ing led down the garden path in many instances. And the church is
brought to a very sad place many times. What a responsibility rests
upon the church leaders today, the ministers and the church officers!
Are you sure Christ is the Head of your church? Are you sure that He is
leading and guiding you, or are you today asking some man to come
and be eyes for you?

Moses made a mistake here, friend. Moses could make mistakes,
by the way. He was a sinner. The interesting thing is that he wrote this;
so he recorded his own mistake. I'm afraid that if some of us had made
these mistakes, we wouldn't have mentioned them.

> **And they departed from the mount of the LORD three
> days' journey: and the ark of the covenant of the LORD
> went before them in the three days' journey, to search
> out a resting place for them.**
>
> **And the cloud of the LORD was upon them by day, when
> they went out of the camp [Num. 10:33–34].**

Now they are on their way. God is leading them. God Himself is
searching out the land. There was no need to have the father-in-law of
Moses do the searching for them.

> **And it came to pass, when the ark set forward, that
> Moses said, Rise up, LORD, and let thine enemies be
> scattered; and let them that hate thee flee before thee.**
>
> **And when it rested, he said, Return, O LORD, unto the
> many thousands of Israel [Num. 10:35–36].**

Apparently Moses followed this ritual of prayer each morning and
every evening when they were on the wilderness march.

CHAPTER 11

THEME: The complaint of the people; the complaint of Moses; God provides quail

The children of Israel now have left Mount Sinai, and chapters 11 and 12 tell of the march from Sinai to Kadesh. We will find that when problems arose, the people fell to murmuring. This was a very serious thing, and it carries important lessons for us.

THE COMPLAINT OF THE PEOPLE

And when the people complained, it displeased the Lord: and the Lord heard it; and his anger was kindled; and the fire of the Lord burnt among them, and consumed them that were in the uttermost parts of the camp [Num. 11:1].

Every time the people complained, the glory of the Lord appeared. He was displeased with their groaning and their complaining.

We can be sure that the Lord is displeased with many of the criticizing, complaining saints today. They are everlastingly finding fault and nothing seems to please them. God doesn't want it that way for you, my friend. He wants you to be a happy, joyful Christian.

And the people cried unto Moses; and when Moses prayed unto the Lord, the fire was quenched.

And he called the name of the place Taberah: because the fire of the Lord burnt among them [Num. 11:2-3].

Now, what is behind all this complaining? Who were the troublemakers? We can locate them here, and we are just as able to locate them today.

**And the mixed multitude that was among them fell
a-lusting: and the children of Israel also wept again,
and said, Who shall give us flesh to eat? [Num. 11:4].**

Who is it that started this? It is the mixed multitude. You will remember that the mixed multitude were those who were not sure who they were. They could not go up and join one of the tribes. They couldn't declare their pedigree. They weren't sure whether they should go on the wilderness march or not. They were the products of mixed marriages. Each of them had one parent back in Egypt and one parent in the camp of Israel. They were Egyptian enough to like Egypt, and they were Israelite enough to want to go on the wilderness march.

We have our churches filled with people like that today. They want to mix with church people and go to church. They want to be moral and live upstanding lives; so they join a church. Then, during the week, they run with the world. They are a mixed multitude. They are not quite sure where they do belong. They are not sure if they are born again—they don't know their pedigree.

I have discovered through my years as a pastor that the real troublemakers in any church are the mixed multitude. They are fellow travelers with the world and with the church people. They like to have a church banquet, but they don't want the Bible study. They don't want to be forward in the march, close to the ark of God; they want to stay way in the back because they are not sure but what they may want to turn and go back some time. They are not quite clear about what they believe. They are never happy when others are having a real time of spiritual blessing. They're uncomfortable in the church, but they are also uncomfortable with the world. They just don't seem to fit in. They are a square peg in a round hole and they are the troublemakers.

Now out here in the wilderness, what do you think they wanted? Listen to them.

**We remember the fish, which we did eat in Egypt freely;
the cucumbers, and the melons, and the leeks, and the
onions, and the garlick:**

But now our soul is dried away: there is nothing at all, beside this manna, before our eyes [Num. 11:5-6].

Notice what they missed. Everything they liked was a condiment, except the fish. They couldn't catch fish out in that wilderness—there weren't any lakes out there. They remembered the fish they had in Egypt. There they had all the fish they wanted. I'm of the opinion that in Egypt they were tired of the fish, but now that is what they remembered. They fell to lusting.

The children of Israel became infected with this complaining, and they began to weep along with the mixed multitude. This was like a spreading, contagious disease which swept through the camp. Before long, the whole crowd was weeping, remembering Egypt.

So they start to complain about the manna. They have the manna to eat, and it is miraculously provided by God every day, but they don't like it.

And the manna was as coriander seed, and the colour thereof as the colour of bdellium.

And the people went about, and gathered it, and ground it in mills, or beat it in a mortar, and baked it in pans, and made cakes of it: and the taste of it was as the taste of fresh oil.

And when the dew fell upon the camp in the night, the manna fell upon it [Num. 11:7-9].

The Spirit of God describes manna for us the second time. The thing they didn't like—how wonderful it was! It was not a monotonous food. The fact of the matter is, as we will see in Deuteronomy, when they went through the wilderness, their feet did not swell. They did not get beriberi from eating the manna. That manna had all the necessary vitamins in it. It was God's food. That manna gave them complete nourishment. Manna, of course, is a picture of the Lord Jesus Christ and of the Word of God which reveals Him.

There were many ways the manna could be prepared. It could be baked or fried; they could grind it to make a bread or a cake out of it. Mrs. Moses probably compiled a cookbook with one hundred and one recipes for manna. The Spirit of God is saying this was an adequate food, a marvelous food, and He is showing to us that it was this food which the children of Israel despised.

Let's not sit back and say how terrible the children of Israel were. How about you, my friend? That manna speaks of Christ. How do you feel about Him? Do you get tired of Him?

Many Christians get tired of manna. A lot of people get tired of Bible study. I think it is safe to say that the largest segment of the church today does not want Bible study. They just won't go for it. The predicament of the church today is due to the fact that folk have turned from the Word and are trying to feed somewhere else other than on the manna which God has provided.

THE COMPLAINT OF MOSES

After this, even Moses gets a little weary of this crowd. I must say that I have a certain sympathy for him.

> Then Moses heard the people weep throughout their families, every man in the door of his tent: and the anger of the LORD was kindled greatly; Moses also was displeased.

> And Moses said unto the LORD, Wherefore hast thou afflicted thy servant? and wherefore have I not found favour in thy sight, that thou layest the burden of all this people upon me?

> Have I conceived all this people? have I begotten them, that thou shouldest say unto me, Carry them in thy bosom, as a nursing father beareth the sucking child, unto the land which thou swarest unto their fathers?

> Whence should I have flesh to give unto all this people?
> for they weep unto me, saying, Give us flesh, that we
> may eat.
>
> I am not able to bear all this people alone, because it is
> too heavy for me.
>
> And if thou deal thus with me, kill me, I pray thee, out
> of hand, if I have found favour in thy sight; and let me
> not see my wretchedness [Num. 11:10-15].

Is Moses complaining? It sounds to me as though he is complaining here. Moses wasn't a perfect man, by any means. He was just a plain human being who was mightily used by God. Moses said he would rather be dead than go through what he was going through with that crowd!

I know pastors who have ulcers and nervous breakdowns. I know several men who have left the ministry. They did the same thing Moses did—complained to the Lord that the burden was too great. They got tired of hearing the criticisms and the complaints and the whining and the difficulties.

> And the Lord said unto Moses, Gather unto me seventy
> men of the elders of Israel, whom thou knowest to be the
> elders of the people, and officers over them; and bring
> them unto the tabernacle of the congregation, that they
> may stand there with thee [Num. 11:16].

Moses made a mistake in complaining like this to God. Moses said that he was the one who was bearing all these people. Well, he wasn't. God never asked him to. God was bearing them and also bearing Moses, but Moses was not fully casting himself upon God. Now God says, "Alright, Moses, I'll give you help if that is what you want." God very patiently, very graciously, provides some assistance for Moses. Seventy elders were appointed.

By the way, these seventy elders continued down through the history of Israel. In the time of our Lord they were called the Sanhedrin. One night they met and decided to put the Lord Jesus to death. I don't think they needed this organization.

We seem to think in the church today that if we will multiply committees and organizations and methods, we will solve our problems. Well, it has not solved our problems. We don't need more organizations; we don't need Sanhedrins.

> **And I will come down and talk with thee there: and I will take of the spirit which is upon thee, and will put it upon them; and they shall bear the burden of the people with thee, that thou bear it not thyself alone [Num. 11:17].**

God had called Moses to lead the people, and God would provide the strength for Moses to do that. God always does. He never asks anyone to do more than he can do. If you feel that you are overworked or that you are doing too much, maybe you really are. Maybe you are doing more than God wants you to do. God will not overburden those who are His own.

> **And say thou unto the people, Sanctify yourselves against to-morrow, and ye shall eat flesh: for ye have wept in the ears of the LORD, saying, Who shall give us flesh to eat? for it was well with us in Egypt: therefore the LORD will give you flesh, and ye shall eat.**
>
> **Ye shall not eat one day, nor two days, nor five days, neither ten days, nor twenty days;**
>
> **But even a whole month, until it come out at your nostrils, and it be loathsome unto you: because that ye have despised the LORD which is among you, and have wept before him, saying, Why came we forth out of Egypt? [Num. 11:18–20].**

It is interesting to read the comment that the Spirit of God makes concerning this incident. Psalm 106 is a historic psalm, and there we read in verse 15, "And he gave them their request; but sent leanness into their soul." God answered their request, but he sent leanness into their soul. I imagine some of them ran around and said they got their answer to prayer, but notice the cost.

We are to make our requests known unto God with thanksgiving (Phil. 4:6), because we know that God is going to hear and answer our prayer. Most of the time God will say no to our prayer, which is the very best answer. Sometimes we pray for things that aren't the best for us. If we beg and complain, God may answer our prayer but give us leanness in our soul.

I remember a certain man who was an official in a church I served years ago. He came to me and asked me to pray for him. His business was shaky, and he wanted me to pray that the Lord would bless his business. He said it offered him the opportunity to become wealthy if he could get it past this critical period. I was a young preacher then, and I went immediately and prayed that the man would make money and that God would establish his business. He prayed for it too. God heard our prayers and the man got rich, which was the worst thing that could have happened to him. He had a fine family until they got more money than they needed. He lost all of his children. God granted their request, but sent leanness to their souls.

God tells Moses that for a whole month they will eat flesh until it becomes loathsome to them. He will do this because they have despised Him and have wept before Him.

> **And Moses said, The people, among whom I am, are six hundred thousand footmen; and thou hast said, I will give them flesh, that they may eat a whole month.**
>
> **Shall the flocks and the herds be slain for them, to suffice them? or shall all the fish of the sea be gathered together for them, to suffice them? [Num. 11:21–22].**

Moses is asking God how He is going to do this.

> And the LORD said unto Moses, Is the LORD's hand waxed
> short? thou shalt see now whether my word shall come
> to pass unto thee or not [Num. 11:23].

God answers him that He will do it. We never need to ask the Lord
how He is going to do something after He says He will do it. He will do
it, and He doesn't need your *how* and my *how*. He does it the way He
wants to do it.

> And Moses went out, and told the people the words of
> the LORD, and gathered the seventy men of the elders of
> the people, and set them round about the tabernacle.
>
> And the LORD came down in a cloud, and spake unto
> him, and took of the spirit that was upon him, and gave
> it unto the seventy elders: and it came to pass, that,
> when the spirit rested upon them, they prophesied, and
> did not cease [Num. 11:24–25].

Notice that there was actually no more power than there had been before. There was a lot more machinery than there was before, but there
was no more power because the same Spirit was divided among them.

> But there remained two of the men in the camp, the
> name of the one was Eldad, and the name of the other
> Medad: and the spirit rested upon them; and they were
> of them that were written, but went not out unto the tab-
> ernacle: and they prophesied in the camp.
>
> And there ran a young man, and told Moses, and said,
> Eldad and Medad do prophesy in the camp.
>
> And Joshua the son of Nun, the servant of Moses, one of
> his young men, answered and said, My lord Moses, for-
> bid them.

And Moses said unto him, Enviest thou for my sake?
would God that all the LORD's people were prophets, and
that the LORD would put his spirit upon them!

And Moses gat him into the camp, he and the elders of
Israel [Num. 11:26–30].

Joshua was very loyal to Moses, and that was wonderful. But even
more wonderful is the revelation that there wasn't a jealous bone in
the body of Moses. He was not jealous because these others were able
to prophesy. I believe there are three great sins in the ministry: lazi-
ness, jealousy, and boredom. Some of us are guilty of all three. We
have seen that Moses was not lazy or bored; now we know he was not
a jealous man either. Jealousy is an awful thing.

GOD PROVIDES QUAIL

And there went forth a wind from the LORD, and brought
quails from the sea, and let them fall by the camp, as it
were a day's journey on this side, and as it were a day's
journey on the other side, round about the camp, and as
it were two cubits high upon the face of the earth [Num.
11:31].

The Lord gives them the meat He promised. He is providing quail on
toast—they couldn't have it better than this! I can't even imagine
quail in abundance like this. I've been quail hunting all day and
found two or three quail.

And the people stood up all that day, and all that night,
and all the next day, and they gathered the quails: he
that gathered least gathered ten homers: and they
spread them all abroad for themselves round about the
camp [Num. 11:32].

That is about eighty-six gallons. They didn't have cold storage; so they had to cook all that. They demonstrated real gluttony.

> **And while the flesh was yet between their teeth, ere it was chewed, the wrath of the LORD was kindled against the people, and the LORD smote the people with a very great plague.**
>
> **And he called the name of that place Kibrothhattaavah: because there they buried the people that lusted.**
>
> **And the people journeyed from Kibrothhattaavah unto Hazeroth; and abode at Hazeroth [Num. 11:33–35].**

God judges those things. He still does. Remember that Paul writes, "For if we would judge ourselves, we should not be judged. But when we are judged, we are chastened of the Lord, that we should not be condemned with the world" (1 Cor. 11:31–32).

CHAPTER 12

THEME: Jealousy of Miriam and Aaron; judgment of Miriam

The Bible tells us very little about the home life of Moses. But from what we do know, I can't believe it could have been very happy. The incident recorded in this chapter is a family matter which occurred during the march from Sinai to Kadesh-barnea. In this chapter we will find rebellion in high places, among the leaders of the children of Israel.

JEALOUSY OF MIRIAM AND AARON

And Miriam and Aaron spake against Moses because of the Ethiopian woman whom he had married: for he had married an Ethiopian woman [Num. 12:1].

I do not think this wife was Zipporah, the daughter of the priest of Midian—she would be a Midianite. The last we heard of Zipporah is when her father brought her to Moses at Mount Sinai (Exod. 18:2). Did she return home with her father? Was she dead? Who is this Ethiopian or Cushite wife? Scripture is silent. All we can say is that this appears to be a second wife. The point here is that Miriam used this marriage as a pretext to protest the authority of Moses.

And they said, Hath the LORD indeed spoken only by Moses? hath he not spoken also by us? And the LORD heard it [Num. 12:2].

This is big sister talking. Miriam could say, "Who does this boy Moses think he is? Why, I can remember when he was a little baby in an ark and I watched over him. If I hadn't watched over him, where would he be today?" And Aaron, the high priest, Moses' big brother, joins in.

(Now the man Moses was very meek, above all the men which were upon the face of the earth) [Num. 12:3].

It is stated of Moses and of our Lord Jesus that they were meek. Remember that meekness is not weakness. Meekness is being obedient to God and doing His will.

And the LORD spake suddenly unto Moses, and unto Aaron, and unto Miriam, Come out ye three unto the tabernacle of the congregation. And they three came out [Num. 12:4].

This is a family affair, you see.

And he said, Hear now my words: If there be a prophet among you, I the LORD will make myself known unto him in a vision, and will speak unto him in a dream.

My servant Moses is not so, who is faithful in all mine house.

With him will I speak mouth to mouth, even apparently, and not in dark speeches; and the similitude of the LORD shall he behold: wherefore then were ye not afraid to speak against my servant Moses?

And the anger of the LORD was kindled against them; and he departed [Num. 12:6–9].

God is saying that He chooses the prophets. Also He says that Moses is greater than the others—he is faithful in all My house. God says that He deals differently with him than with any other prophet: He speaks with Moses directly.

I think we find this to be true as we study the Old Testament. I cannot find that He dealt with any other prophet as He dealt with

Moses. God appeared in dreams to Abraham. He appeared in dreams to Joseph. But God dealt with Moses face to face. Moses is different from all the others. Later on we will see that God says, "I will raise them up a Prophet from among their brethren, like unto thee, and will put my words in his mouth; and he shall speak unto them all that I shall command him" (Deut. 18:18). That Prophet who would be like unto Moses is the Lord Jesus Christ.

JUDGMENT OF MIRIAM

And the cloud departed from off the tabernacle; and, behold, Miriam became leprous, white as snow: and Aaron looked upon Miriam, and, behold, she was leprous [Num. 12:10].

They had been very foolish in what they had said. Miriam became leprous which was God's severe judgment on her. Moses prayed to the Lord for her—how forgiving and gracious Moses was! Although God healed her, she had to be shut out from the camp for seven days, and the people could not journey while she was shut out of the camp. She held up the march for a whole week.

And Miriam was shut out from the camp seven days: and the people journeyed not till Miriam was brought in again.

And afterward the people removed from Hazeroth, and pitched in the wilderness of Paran [Num. 12:15–16].

Why wasn't Aaron struck with the leprosy? Because Aaron was God's high priest. If he were a leper he could not serve in that capacity; Israel would have had no intercessor to stand between them and God. So God didn't use this family affair to judge Aaron at this time. It was Aaron who pleaded with Moses, ". . . Alas, my lord, I beseech thee, lay not the sin upon us, wherein we have done foolishly, and wherein we have sinned" (Num. 12:11). The judgment was caused by the jealousy in both of them, but Miriam was the leader in it. Her name is mentioned first, and the verb *spake* in verse 1 is in the feminine— "she spoke." Aaron was not a leader; he was a follower. He was weak and pliable, a characteristic we see in Exodus 32 regarding the making of the golden calf. The sins of jealousy and envy were nurtured in Miriam's heart, and God rightly judged her.

CHAPTER 13

THEME: Sending spies; choice of spies; commission of spies; conduct of spies; confirmation of facts; misinterpretation of facts; right interpretation of facts

Israel has reached Kadesh-barnea, which borders the Promised Land. It is sad to see that Kadesh becomes their Waterloo because of their unbelief.

This chapter includes the cause of their sending spies, the choice of the spies, the commission of the spies, the conduct of the spies, the spies' confirmation of the facts, and the two interpretations of those facts—a majority and a minority report.

SENDING SPIES

And the LORD spake unto Moses, saying,

Send thou men, that they may search the land of Canaan, which I give unto the children of Israel: of every tribe of their fathers shall ye send a man, every one a ruler among them.

And Moses by the commandment of the LORD sent them from the wilderness of Paran: all those men were heads of the children of Israel [Num. 13:1–3].

Whose idea was it to send in the spies? Was it the idea of God? Was it His thought to spy out the land? No. We always need to get a composite picture from the Word of God, because many times one facet will be given in one place and another facet given in another place. As an example, we need all four of the Gospel records to have a total spectrum of the Lord Jesus Christ. Although we get the impression here that this is God's idea, we find that He was responding to their request. Listen to the account in Deuteronomy: "And I said unto you, Ye are come unto the mountain of the Amorites, which the LORD our God doth give unto us. Behold, the LORD thy God hath set the land before thee: go up and possess it, as the LORD God of thy fathers hath said unto thee; fear not, neither be discouraged. And ye came near unto me every one of you, and said, We will send men before us, and they shall search us out the land, and bring us word again by what way we must go up, and into what cities we shall come" (Deut. 1:20–22). It was not God's idea to send spies into the land. The sending in of the spies denoted a weakness and a fear on the part of the people. There was a fear that maybe they wouldn't be able to take the land. It was so easy for them to rationalize and decide on spies as a matter of wisdom.

However, God is leading Israel to the land He has promised them. Their request for spies reveals a lack of faith on their part. They are not trusting Him. God had already been in and spied out the land. He knew all about it. He would not have sent them into the land unless He knew they could take it. When they finally did enter the land, the giants were still there; all the difficulties and problems were still there, yet they took the land.

What an important message this is for us today! Are we really walking by faith? Of course we need to take precautions, but there is a time when we do need to commit our way unto the Lord. "Commit thy way unto the LORD; trust also in him; and he shall bring it to pass" (Ps. 37:5). You and I need to come to the place in our lives when we commit our way to Him and trust Him completely.

These folk have come to that place but they're not trusting God. They decide to send out spies to find out what lay ahead of them. We find this to be another instance where God yields to the desires of His people. He permits them to do this thing. It was said of them later, ". . . He gave them their request; but sent leanness into their soul" (Ps. 106:15). This time it will be worse than leanness.

After they demonstrate their lack of faith and lack of trust in God, He orders the spy mission, in response to their request, and commands that it should be done in a fair and orderly way, and that a ruler from each tribe go as a spy.

CHOICE OF SPIES

The list of the spies is given here. We are especially interested in two of them.

Of the tribe of Judah, Caleb the son of Jephunneh.

Of the tribe of Ephraim, Oshea the son of Nun [Num. 13:6, 8].

Oshea or Hoshea is Joshua. We will hear more of these two remarkable men who brought in the minority report.

COMMISSION OF SPIES

And Moses sent them to spy out the land of Canaan, and said unto them, Get you up this way southward, and go up into the mountain:

And see the land, what it is; and the people that dwelleth therein, whether they be strong or weak, few or many;

And what the land is that they dwell in, whether it be good or bad; and what cities they be that they dwell in, whether in tents, or in strong holds;

And what the land is, whether it be fat or lean, whether there be wood therein, or not. And be ye of good courage, and bring of the fruit of the land. Now the time was the time of the firstripe grapes [Num. 13:17–20].

Now the spies are to go in. They have been given their commission and they know what they are to do.

CONDUCT OF SPIES

So they went up, and searched the land from the wilderness of Zin unto Rehob, as men come to Hamath [Num. 13:21].

Hamath is way up in the extreme north of the land. The spies did a thorough job. The fact of the matter is that they could have written a book entitled *Inside the Promised Land*. They knew a great deal about it. We are told the places they went and that they saw the children of Anak. These were giants.

> **And they ascended by the south, and came unto Hebron; where Ahiman, Sheshai, and Talmai, the children of Anak, were. (Now Hebron was built seven years before Zoan in Egypt.)**
>
> **And they came unto the brook of Eshcol, and cut down from thence a branch with one cluster of grapes, and they bare it between two upon a staff; and they brought of the pomegranates, and of the figs.**
>
> **The place was called the brook Eshcol, because of the cluster of grapes which the children of Israel cut down from thence.**
>
> **And they returned from searching of the land after forty days [Num. 13:22–25].**

Our translation gives the impression that it took two men to carry one bunch of grapes. At least they cut down enough grapes (and they were lush grapes) for two men to carry, and it was put on a pole between them. They brought back samples of the fruit to show what a wonderful land it was.

CONFIRMATION OF FACTS

> **And they went and came to Moses, and to Aaron, and to all the congregation of the children of Israel, unto the wilderness of Paran, to Kadesh; and brought back word unto them, and unto all the congregation, and shewed them the fruit of the land.**

> And they told him, and said, We came unto the land
> whither thou sentest us, and surely it floweth with milk
> and honey; and this is the fruit of it [Num. 13:26-27].

Their report confirmed that God was accurate when He said it was a
land flowing with milk and honey.

MISINTERPRETATION OF FACTS

> Nevertheless the people be strong that dwell in the land,
> and the cities are walled, and very great: and moreover
> we saw the children of Anak there.

> The Amalekites dwell in the land of the south: and the
> Hittites, and the Jebusites, and the Amorites, dwell in
> the mountains: and the Canaanites dwell by the sea, and
> by the coast of Jordan [Num. 13:28-29].

This all was true. There were giants in the land. The cities were
walled and very great. They were right in their facts, but they misin-
terpreted the facts. That is where they went awry.

> But the men that went up with him said, We be not able
> to go up against the people; for they are stronger than
> we.

> And they brought up an evil report of the land which
> they had searched unto the children of Israel, saying,
> The land, through which we have gone to search it, is a
> land that eateth up the inhabitants thereof; and all the
> people that we saw in it are men of a great stature.

> And there we saw the giants, the sons of Anak, which
> come of the giants: and we were in our own sight as
> grasshoppers, and so we were in their sight [Num.
> 13:31-33].

When you are afraid and you have lost your faith, difficulties and problems are magnified. They become greater than they really are. There were giants, but the men thought they were bigger than they actually were. They looked bigger because these men were afraid. What an interesting contrast they give us here. Giants and grasshoppers! Do you know what they left out? They forgot to include God! They compared themselves to the giants as grasshoppers. That is the way they saw themselves. They left God out of the picture. If only they had put Him in, what a different story it would have been.

RIGHT INTERPRETATION OF FACTS

And Caleb stilled the people before Moses, and said, Let us go up at once, and possess it; for we are well able to overcome it [Num. 13:30].

Here is the minority report. Caleb spoke up with this report but the other men refuted him. Only Joshua agreed with Caleb.

So there we have the whole picture. The report was accurate as to the facts. But there were two different opinions in the interpretation of those facts. The minority report was "Let's go in and take the land. We are well able to do it." The majority report was, "We can't do it." The people believed the majority report. They didn't believe they could take the land because they lacked faith in God.

CHAPTER 14

THEME: Israel's refusal to enter the land; Moses pleads for Israel; God's judgment; Israel defeated by Amalekites and Canaanites

Israel has not come to the place of decision. They must decide whether they are going to enter the land or not. We find Israel refusing to enter. The reason is their unbelief. The Bible is its own best commentary, and it is the writer to the Hebrews who puts it just that way. "But with whom was he grieved forty years? was it not with them that had sinned, whose carcases fell in the wilderness? And to whom sware he that they should not enter into his rest, but to them that believed not? So we see that they could not enter in because of unbelief" (Heb. 3:17–19). It was unbelief that kept them from going into the land!

ISRAEL'S REFUSAL TO ENTER THE LAND

And all the congregation lifted up their voice, and cried; and the people wept that night.

And all the children of Israel murmured against Moses and against Aaron: and the whole congregation said unto them, Would God that we had died in the land of Egypt! or would God we had died in this wilderness! [Num. 14:1–2].

I am of the opinion that poor Moses and Aaron at this time were wishing they *had* died in the wilderness so they would be rid of their continual complaining.

And wherefore hath the LORD brought us unto this land, to fall by the sword, that our wives and our children

should be a prey? were it not better for us to return into
Egypt? [Num. 14:3].

They are in such a bad frame of mind that they say, "Our wives and
children will be a prey!" They are using their children as an excuse,
pretending they are thinking of the safety of their children, but actually it is a reflection on God. They are saying that God did not care
what happened to their children.

Do you know who it was that entered the land? It was these
children—that next generation. The old folks sat there and cried and
said they were thinking of the safety of the children. The fact of the
matter is that God was thinking of the safety of the children, and He
brought them into the land.

And they said one to another, Let us make a captain,
and let us return into Egypt.

Then Moses and Aaron fell on their faces before all the
assembly of the congregation of the children of Israel.

And Joshua the son of Nun, and Caleb the son of Jephunneh, which were of them that searched the land, rent
their clothes:

And they spake unto all the company of the children of
Israel, saying, The land, which we passed through to
search it, is an exceeding good land.

If the LORD delight in us, then he will bring us into this
land, and give it us; a land which floweth with milk and
honey.

Only rebel not ye against the LORD, neither fear ye the
people of the land; for they are bread for us: their de-
fence is departed from them, and the LORD is with us:
fear them not [Num. 14:4–9].

These two men, Caleb and Joshua, brought the same facts as the
others. What is the difference in their report? The difference is in their

interpretation of the facts because they included God. When you see yourself as a grasshopper in the presence of giants, that is when you need God. These people certainly needed God. Caleb and Joshua insisted that if God would delight in them, He would bring them into the land. But how can God delight in them unless they believe God? They must trust Him.

"They are bread for us" in our idiom would be like saying, "Those people in the land will be 'duck soup' for us!" How can they be so confident? They have faith in God!

> But all the congregation bade stone them with stones. And the glory of the LORD appeared in the tabernacle of the congregation before all the children of Israel [Num. 14:10].

Have you noticed that every time there is a rebellion, or murmuring, or complaining, the glory of the Lord appears? God is highly displeased with this rebellion against Him.

> And the LORD said unto Moses, How long will this people provoke me? and how long will it be ere they believe me, for all the signs which I have shewed among them?

> I will smite them with the pestilence, and disinherit them, and will make of thee a greater nation and mightier than they [Num. 14:11-12].

God is saying, "I'll destroy them and make a nation from you to fulfill My promises."

MOSES PLEADS FOR ISRAEL

> And Moses said unto the LORD, Then the Egyptians shall hear it, (for thou broughtest up this people in thy might from among them;)

And they will tell it to the inhabitants of this land: for they have heard that thou LORD art among this people, that thou LORD art seen face to face, and that thy cloud standeth over them, and that thou goest before them, by day time in a pillar of cloud, and in a pillar of fire by night.

Now if thou shalt kill all this people as one man, then the nations which have heard the fame of thee will speak, saying,

Because the LORD was not able to bring this people into the land which he sware unto them, therefore he hath slain them in the wilderness.

And now, I beseech thee, let the power of my LORD be great, according as thou hast spoken, saying,

The LORD is longsuffering, and of great mercy, forgiving iniquity and transgression, and by no means clearing the guilty, visiting the iniquity of the fathers upon the children unto the third and fourth generation.

Pardon, I beseech thee, the iniquity of this people according unto the greatness of thy mercy, and as thou hast forgiven this people, from Egypt even until now [Num. 14:13–19].

Moses reminds God that the rumor will go around that although He was able to bring them out of Egypt, He was not able to put them into the land, to complete that which He had begun. God agrees to go ahead with them and put Israel into the land.

And the LORD said, I have pardoned according to thy word [Num. 14:20].

And then the Lord gives this prophecy:

> But as truly as I live, all the earth shall be filled with the glory of the LORD [Num. 14:21].

As God brought these children of Israel out of the land of Egypt and did put them in the Promised Land, so God will complete the plan He had for you when He saved you. And He will complete the plan He is working on now for the entire earth, because the time is coming when the whole earth shall be filled with the glory of the Lord.

GOD'S JUDGMENT

> Because all those men which have seen my glory, and my miracles, which I did in Egypt and in the wilderness, and have tempted me now these ten times, and have not hearkened to my voice;
>
> Surely they shall not see the land which I sware unto their fathers, neither shall any of them that provoked me see it:
>
> But my servant Caleb, because he had another spirit with him, and hath followed me fully, him will I bring into the land whereinto he went; and his seed shall possess it [Num. 14:22-24].

Judgment falls on the children of Israel. The generation that murmured will not enter the Promised Land. Joshua and Caleb are the only ones whom God singles out from the people. God promises that they shall enter the land, and God made good that promise.

> Your carcases shall fall in this wilderness; and all that were numbered of you, according to your whole number, from twenty years old and upward, which have murmured against me,
>
> Doubtless ye shall not come into the land, concerning which I sware to make you dwell therein, save Caleb the son of Jephunneh, and Joshua the son of Nun.

> But your little ones, which ye said should be a prey, them will I bring in, and they shall know the land which ye have despised.
>
> But as for you, your carcases, they shall fall in this wilderness [Num. 14:29–32].

Their children, that they implied God did not care about, would be brought safely into the land they had despised.

> And your children shall wander in the wilderness forty years, and bear your whoredoms, until your carcases be wasted in the wilderness.
>
> After the number of the days in which ye searched the land, even forty days, each day for a year, shall ye bear your iniquities, even forty years, and ye shall know my breach of promise.
>
> I the LORD have said, I will surely do it unto all this evil congregation, that are gathered together against me: in this wilderness they shall be consumed, and there they shall die [Num. 14:33–35].

God tells them that they will wander in the wilderness for forty years—one year for each day the spies were in the land.

> And the men, which Moses sent to search the land, who returned, and made all the congregation to murmur against him, by bringing up a slander upon the land,
>
> Even those men that did bring up the evil report upon the land, died by the plague before the LORD [Num. 14:36–37].

The ten spies who brought the evil report and led in the rebellion died of a plague.

ISRAEL DEFEATED BY AMALEKITES
AND CANAANITES

**And Moses told these sayings unto all the children of
Israel: and the people mourned greatly [Num. 14:39].**

They had turned from the land, but as they face the wilderness, they
are actually more afraid of the wilderness than they had been afraid of
entering the land.

**And they rose up early in the morning, and gat them up
into the top of the mountain, saying, Lo, we be here, and
will go up unto the place which the LORD hath promised: for we have sinned.**

**And Moses said, Wherefore now do ye transgress the
commandment of the LORD? but it shall not prosper.**

**Go not up, for the LORD is not among you; that ye be not
smitten before your enemies [Num. 14:40–42].**

They had lost their opportunity. They would not go up into the land
when God wanted them to go. Now they presume to go up. This is
presumption. Faith is not presumption! They again want to go their
way rather than God's way. There can be no victory when there is no
submission to the will of God.

**But they presumed to go up unto the hill top: neverthe-
less the ark of the covenant of the LORD, and Moses, departed not out of the camp.**

**Then the Amalekites came down, and the Canaanites
which dwelt in that hill, and smote them, and discom-
fited them, even unto Hormah [Num. 14:44–45].**

CHAPTER 15

THEME: God's purpose is not destroyed; death penalty for breaking the sabbath; the ribband of blue

We have seen that the children of Moses had come to a point of decision at Kadesh-barnea. As you know, decisions are the difficult things for all of us in this life. This is especially true for the Christian. Many times we come to the crossroad and we are sure which way to go. But it was crystal clear to these people which way they should have gone. They faced the choice of entering the land by faith or turning back into the wilderness in unbelief. They made the wrong decision and turned in unbelief.

However, when they looked at the wilderness, they changed their mind and decided that the Promised Land with its walled cities and giants was not so bad as the wilderness; so they attempted to go into the land. This was not a decision of faith; it was a decision based on their experience of two years in the wilderness. They presumed to go into the land. Presumption is as dangerous as unbelief.

A businessman of my acquaintance had a responsible position, then was laid off from this position shortly after he had bought a new home and new furniture. His question to me was: "Why would God let this happen to me since He had led me to buy the house and furniture?" I told him, "I remember that while you were looking for the new house, you mentioned that you were not sure of the leading of God at that time and you specifically mentioned that you didn't like the area, yet you bought the house. Now you are blaming God for all of it. Could it be that you moved by presumption rather than by faith?" He said, "Well, I just thought God would bless me."

My friend, we need to be extremely careful whether we are moving by faith or by presumption. Somewhere between these two is the will of God. It is important to spend time waiting upon the Lord to find out what is His will.

Now we enter that division of the Book of Numbers from chapters 15 to 25, which I call "Faltering, Fumbling, and Fussing through the Wilderness." At Kadesh-barnea, God has turned them back into the wilderness. Walking is turned to wandering; marching is turned to murmuring; witnessing is turned to wailing; warring is turned to wobbling; singing is turned to sighing, and working is turned to wishing.

Unfortunately, I must say that a great many Christians go through life just like that!

Now, the interesting thing is that these are silent years. There is no record of them anywhere. We are given only a few incidents with no connected history. However, we are given indications of the general characteristics of those years. In chapter 33, which is about as uninteresting as any chapter could be, we will find the log of the journeys. We can fit the recorded incidents into this log, but it shows us that we are not given a detailed account of those years. The years are *wasted* years for the children of Israel.

When we get to Joshua, chapter 5, we will learn that they did not circumcise their children during this period. This shows that they were not fulfilling the will of God relative to the covenant which God had made to Abraham. We also know that they did not offer sacrifices to God. "Have ye offered unto me sacrifices and offerings in the wilderness forty years, O house of Israel?" (Amos 5:25). These sacrifices pointed to Christ, and they were not offering them during the forty years. Not only that, but we also know they worshiped idols during this period. "But ye have borne the tabernacle of your Moloch and Chiun your images, the star of your god, which ye made to yourselves" (Amos 5:26). Stephen relates this again in Acts, "Then God turned, and gave them up to worship the host of heaven; as it is written in the book of the prophets, O ye house of Israel, have ye offered to me slain beasts and sacrifices by the space of forty years in the wilderness? Yea, ye took up the tabernacle of Moloch, and the star of your god Remphan, figures which ye made to worship them: and I will carry you away beyond Babylon" (Acts 7:42–43). So we see that the children of Israel were not faithful to God during this period.

These years of wandering have many lessons for us today. We are pilgrims and strangers in this world. In God's sight the world today is a wilderness. It may not look that way to us. Down here in Southern California, we have never felt this was a wilderness, but God sees it as a wilderness. You and I, believers, are just passing through this world. We are strangers and pilgrims.

Let me emphasize again: the whole theme of this chapter is that they can delay God's blessing but they cannot destroy God's purpose. Notice that although the children of Israel have turned back into the wilderness, God says they will enter the land, and as far as God is concerned, it is as good as done. That is the reason a great deal of prophecy is stated in what is known as the "prophetic tense" in the Old Testament. It is stated in the past tense although it speaks of a future event. You see, friends, as far as God is concerned, when He says something is going to come to pass, it has already come to pass in His program.

GOD'S PURPOSE IS NOT DESTROYED

And the LORD spake unto Moses, saying,

Speak unto the children of Israel, and say unto them, When ye be come into the land of your habitations, which I give unto you [Num. 15:1-2].

God is now telling them things which they are to do when they enter the land. Forty years later, Israel in a new generation entered the land and they did the things which their fathers neglected to do.

And will make an offering by fire unto the LORD, a burnt offering, or a sacrifice in performing a vow, or in a free-will offering, or in your solemn feasts, to make a sweet savour unto the LORD, of the herd, or of the flock:

Then shall he that offereth his offering unto the LORD bring a meat offering of a tenth deal of flour mingled with the fourth part of an hin of oil [Num. 15:3-4].

Now God goes on to talk to them about this offering. A hin of oil was to be put on it, which speaks of the Holy Spirit. Then there was to be the fourth part of a hin of wine for a drink offering, and that speaks of joy. Notice how God says, "When thou prepares a bullock" (v. 8). God talks to them about what they will do in the land as definitely as if it were done. Although this generation in the wilderness will turn back to idolatry, the new generation that is coming into the land will offer these offerings which all speak of the person of the Lord Jesus Christ.

My friend, how is it with you today? Probably on Sunday you go to church and your thoughts center on the Bible and the Lord Jesus Christ. But what happens to you upon Monday when you go out into the wilderness of the world? Do you join in the idolatry of the world? Do you serve the gods of this world? Do you live a sacred, religious life on Sunday and a secular life during the rest of the week? I tell you, the Lord Jesus wants to go into the market place with you. He wants to go on the streets of this world and into the trading places with you. He is as real there as He is in the church on Sunday.

Now he mentions something which we have previously seen in Leviticus, the offering for sins of ignorance.

> **Then it shall be, if ought be committed by ignorance without the knowledge of the congregation, that all the congregation shall offer one young bullock for a burnt offering, for a sweet savour unto the LORD, with his meat offering, and his drink offering, according to the manner, and one kid of the goats for a sin offering.**

> **And the priest shall make an atonement for all the congregation of the children of Israel, and it shall be forgiven them; for it is ignorance: and they shall bring their offering, a sacrifice made by fire unto the LORD, and their sin offering before the LORD, for their ignorance:**

> **And it shall be forgiven all the congregation of the children of Israel, and the stranger that sojourneth among**

them; seeing all the people were in ignorance [Num. 15:24–26].

Sins of ignorance remind us of a current issue. There is a great deal of debate about whether the heathen, who have never heard the gospel, are lost. May I say to you, they are not lost because they are ignorant of the gospel. They are lost because they are sinners. Sins of ignorance had to have an offering. So men are lost because they are sinners, whether or not they have heard the gospel. I believe every man should have the opportunity to hear the gospel and to make a decision, but men are lost long before they hear and reject the gospel. Jesus Christ came to seek and to save that which was lost, and all men are lost. That is their natural state. Lost mankind is not sitting down in grief today because they have not heard the gospel. If you have ever had the opportunity of taking the gospel to those who have never heard it, you will recognize that they are not anxious to hear it.

DEATH PENALTY FOR BREAKING THE SABBATH

One incident that happened during the wilderness wanderings is startling to read.

And while the children of Israel were in the wilderness, they found a man that gathered sticks upon the sabbath day.

And they that found him gathering sticks brought him unto Moses and Aaron, and unto all the congregation.

And they put him in ward, because it was not declared what should be done to him.

And the LORD said unto Moses, The man shall be surely put to death: all the congregation shall stone him with stones without the camp.

And all the congregation brought him without the camp, and stoned him with stones, and he died; as the LORD commanded Moses [Num. 15:32–36].

This is very severe. This makes one thing very clear. The death penalty was the penalty for breaking any of the Ten Commandments. We need to see this to understand what it means that the Lord Jesus Christ died our death for us.

THE RIBBAND OF BLUE

And the LORD spake unto Moses, saying,

Speak unto the children of Israel, and bid them that they make them fringes in the borders of their garments throughout their generations, and that they put upon the fringe of the borders a ribband of blue:

And it shall be unto you for a fringe, that ye may look upon it, and remember all the commandments of the LORD, and do them; and that ye seek not after your own heart and your own eyes, after which ye use to go a-whoring:

That ye may remember, and do all my commandments, and be holy unto your God.

I am the LORD your God, which brought you out of the land of Egypt, to be your God: I am the LORD your God [Num. 15:37–41].

That border of blue, which is a heavenly color, was to remind them of the fact that they were God's people and they were to have a heavenly walk down here on this earth. There are many believers today who need to have that "border of blue" to remind them that as God's children they are set apart and are to live for the Lord Jesus Christ.

CHAPTER 16

THEME: Rebellion against divinely constituted author-ity; the sixth murmuring

Although we have no detailed account of the children of Israel dur-ing these wasted years in the wilderness, there are isolated inci-dents recorded. From chapters 16 through 19, we have four incidents which all concern the priesthood. Chapter 16 is the gainsaying of Korah. Chapter 17 is about Aaron's rod that budded. Chapter 18 is the confirmation of the priesthood, and chapter 19 concerns the offering of the red heifer.

REBELLION AGAINST DIVINELY CONSTITUTED AUTHORITY

This chapter opens with the murmuring of the children of Israel. This is the fifth murmuring, and before we get out of the chapter, we will find the sixth murmuring. One can divide the wandering of the children of Israel according to their murmurings in the wilderness. This one is a murmuring among the priesthood. In fact, it is led by Korah, a very prominent Levite.

> Now Korah, the son of Izhar, the son of Kohath, the son of Levi, and Dathan and Abiram, the sons of Eliab, and On, the son of Peleth, sons of Reuben, took men:
>
> And they rose up before Moses, with certain of the chil-dren of Israel, two hundred and fifty princes of the as-sembly, famous in the congregation, men of renown:
>
> And they gathered themselves together against Moses and against Aaron, and said unto them, Ye take too much upon you, seeing all the congregation are holy,

**every one of them, and the LORD is among them: where-
fore then lift ye up yourselves above the congregation of
the LORD? [Num. 16:1-3].**

Korah was a Levite of great authority. Associated with him were 250 of
the princes of the assembly who were also men of authority. A rebellion, to be effective, must have prominent men behind it. It takes
brains and money. This rebellion was no small affair.

Maybe you thought that protest movements and marches were
new. They are not new at all. Here is a protest movement against the
establishment. These are men of ability and, as always, they appeal to
the mob by making charges such as: "Your rights are being infringed
upon. Your leaders are assuming too much authority. You are being
deprived of something you should have."

Now, actually, the charges made in this rebellion were not true to
the facts. They were absolutely unfounded. Moses was not taking too
much upon himself. If we go back in his history, we find that when
God called him, he refused. He didn't feel capable of leading these
people. Even after God had trained him in the wilderness, he didn't
want the job. He asked for a helper, and God gave him Aaron. Moses
was the meekest man on earth. When Joshua wanted to silence the
prophets, Moses said that he wished all of God's people might prophesy. He didn't have a jealous bone in his body. My friend, we have
seen that Moses was not sinless, but he certainly was not guilty of
taking too much upon himself.

What was really the root trouble here? It was the jealousy of Korah.
This matter of jealousy is an awful thing. All authority is God-given.
No man takes this honor upon himself. God had given the places in
the camp, and He had given the Levites their specific jobs to do. Korah
was a Kohathite, and their position and service were God-appointed.
Moses had his position and duties. Frankly, a rebellion like this must
be dealt with, and extreme measures are going to be used.

This is so important for us to see today. Churches everywhere are
having problems. We are a problem-conscious people today because
we do have problems. My experience is that a great deal of the prob-

lem in churches today and a great deal of rebellion among the people in the churches can be found rooted in one thing—jealousy! This is why the Bible enjoins us to walk in meekness and in lowliness of mind. We are to walk in humility. We are to recognize that all authority is God-given.

In 1 Corinthians 12, Paul pictures the church as a body, a human body. As the body has many members, so the church has many members. When God saves you, He puts you in the body by the baptism of the Holy Spirit. You are to function in a certain way in the body of believers. There are many gifts of the Spirit. If you are a Christian, you have been given a gift, and you are to use that gift as you function in the body of believers. The whole body is not a tongue. Therefore, everyone will not speak in tongues. Not all the body is an eye, nor is all the body an ear. Every individual has a gift and there are many gifts. One of those gifts is the gift of helps, and I can think of hundreds of ways in which you can help to get out the Word of God.

Every believer has a gift, and God wants us to function by exercising that gift. Your business is not to try to get someone else's office or job. We have too much insane vanity among Christians wanting to be chairman of a board or to do something publicly. My friend, most of the members of the body are not seen. We cover them or they are inside the body. Yet their function is essential to the body. It is just so in the church!

Jealousy motivates a great many people who are troublemakers in our churches. These people push themselves into a place of leadership. They attempt to usurp a gift which they do not have at all. They have no particular ability to do the thing that they are attempting. God never called them to do that. That is hurting the church today.

God is going to deal with this rebellion in a definite way. I tell you, the judgment of these men is going to be serious. Let us notice what God did.

And when Moses heard it, he fell upon his face:

And he spake unto Korah and unto all his company, saying, Even to-morrow the LORD will shew who are his,

and who is holy; and will cause him to come near unto him: even him whom he hath chosen will he cause to come near unto him.

This do; Take you censers, Korah, and all his company;

And put fire therein, and put incense in them before the LORD to-morrow: and it shall be that the man whom the LORD doth choose, he shall be holy: ye take too much upon you, ye sons of Levi [Num. 16:4–7].

They had said to Moses and Aaron that they took too much upon themselves. Now Moses is telling them from God that they take too much on themselves.

And Moses said unto Korah, Hear, I pray you, ye sons of Levi:

Seemeth it but a small thing unto you, that the God of Israel hath separated you from the congregation of Israel, to bring you near to himself to do the service of the tabernacle of the LORD, and to stand before the congregation to minister unto them?

And he hath brought thee near to him, and all thy brethren the sons of Levi with thee: and seek ye the priesthood also?

For which cause both thou and all thy company are gathered together against the LORD: and what is Aaron, that ye murmur against him? [Num. 16:8–11].

Because the duties of Moses and Aaron were appointed by God, the murmuring is actually directed at God.

And Moses sent to call Dathan and Abiram, the sons of Eliab: which said, We will not come up:

Is it a small thing that thou hast brought us up out of a land that floweth with milk and honey, to kill us in the wilderness, except thou make thyself altogether a prince over us?

Moreover thou hast not brought us into a land that floweth with milk and honey, or given us inheritance of fields and vineyards: wilt thou put out the eyes of these men? we will not come up [Num. 16:12–14].

Their malicious charge against Moses ignores the fact that had they followed his leadership at Kadesh-barnea, by now they would be settled in the land of milk and honey.

And Moses was very wroth, and said unto the LORD, Respect not thou their offering: I have not taken one ass from them, neither have I hurt one of them.

And Moses said unto Korah, Be thou and all thy company before the LORD, thou, and they, and Aaron, tomorrow:

And take every man his censer, and put incense in them, and bring ye before the LORD every man his censer, two hundred and fifty censers; thou also, and Aaron, each of you his censer [Num. 16:15–17].

It is up to God to make known His will in this matter.

And they took every man his censer, and put fire in them, and laid incense thereon, and stood in the door of the tabernacle of the congregation with Moses and Aaron.

And Korah gathered all the congregation against them unto the door of the tabernacle of the congregation: and the glory of the LORD appeared unto all the congregation.

> And the LORD spake unto Moses and unto Aaron, saying,
>
> Separate yourselves from among this congregation, that I may consume them in a moment [Num. 16:18–21].

Every man took his censer, put incense in it, and came to the tabernacle. We will see that the glory of the Lord appeared. We have noticed before that the glory of the Lord appeared at the time of the murmuring, and now it appears at this time of rebellion.

> And they fell upon their faces, and said, O God, the God of the spirits of all flesh, shall one man sin, and wilt thou be wroth with all the congregation? [Num. 16:22].

Again Moses intercedes for his people.

> And the LORD spake unto Moses, saying,
>
> Speak unto the congregation, saying, Get you up from about the tabernacle of Korah, Dathan, and Abiram.
>
> And Moses rose up and went unto Dathan and Abiram; and the elders of Israel followed him.
>
> And he spake unto the congregation, saying, Depart, I pray you, from the tents of these wicked men, and touch nothing of theirs, lest ye be consumed in all their sins.
>
> So they gat up from the tabernacle of Korah, Dathan, and Abiram, on every side: and Dathan and Abiram came out, and stood in the door of their tents, and their wives, and their sons, and their little children.
>
> And Moses said, Hereby ye shall know that the LORD hath sent me to do all these works; for I have not done them of mine own mind.

> If these men die the common death of all men, or if they
> be visited after the visitation of all men; then the LORD
> hath not sent me.
>
> But if the LORD make a new thing, and the earth open
> her mouth, and swallow them up, with all that apper-
> tain unto them, and they go down quick into the pit;
> then ye shall understand that these men have provoked
> the LORD [Num. 16:23–30].

It is a terrible thing for a man or group of men to disobey God and His
divinely appointed leaders. It is a terrible thing to set up a little system of worship and so divide the people of God. God must deal with
this kind of rebellion, and He must judge it.

> And it came to pass, as he had made an end of speaking
> all these words, that the ground clave asunder that was
> under them:
>
> And the earth opened her mouth, and swallowed them
> up, and their houses, and all the men that appertained
> unto Korah, and all their goods.
>
> They, and all that appertained to them, went down
> alive into the pit, and the earth closed upon them: and
> they perished from among the congregation [Num.
> 16:31–33].

It is awesome to see the way God judged them. Because they attempted to divide the people, God judges them in the same way in
which they had sinned. He divides the people to separate them from
Korah and his group, and then He divides the earth and it closes upon
them. Galatians 6:7 says, "Be not deceived; God is not mocked: for
whatsoever a man soweth, that shall he also reap." God judges the
very same way in which the man sins. That was true of old Jacob; it
was true of David; it was true of Paul, the apostle; and it will be true of
you and me.

And all Israel that were round about them fled at the cry of them: for they said, Lest the earth swallow us up also.

And there came out a fire from the LORD, and consumed the two hundred and fifty men that offered incense [Num. 16:34–35].

These men had been leaders in Israel. They felt they should have had more prominence in their service. What a warning for us today! Too many people have a marvelous gift for serving God, but it would put them into some humble service, and they have the impression they should be running the church. Do you remember Dorcas who had the gift of sewing? That gift was so important to the early church that God used Peter to raise her from the dead. I think that today we need fewer voices trying to do the speaking and more people who will do the tasks such as sewing. We need people to do the humble tasks around the church today. Each and every gift is important. Jealousy and rebellion will be judged by God.

And the LORD spake unto Moses, saying,

Speak unto Eleazar the son of Aaron the priest, that he take up the censers out of the burning, and scatter thou the fire yonder; for they are hallowed.

The censers of these sinners against their own souls, let them make them broad plates for a covering of the altar: for they offered them before the LORD, therefore they are hallowed: and they shall be a sign unto the children of Israel.

And Eleazar the priest took the brasen censers, wherewith they that were burnt had offered; and they were made broad plates for a covering of the altar:

To be a memorial unto the children of Israel, that no stranger, which is not of the seed of Aaron, come near to offer incense before the LORD; that he be not as Korah,

**and as his company: as the Lord said to him by the hand
of Moses [Num. 16:36–40].**

Now God told Moses that the censers of the rebels should be molded
into broad plates for covering of the altar. These were to be a memorial
to the children of Israel that no one was to offer incense before the
Lord unless he was in the line of Aaron, the priest.

THE SIXTH MURMURING

**But on the morrow all the congregation of the children
of Israel murmured against Moses and against Aaron,
saying, Ye have killed the people of the Lord.**

**And it came to pass, when the congregation was gath-
ered against Moses and against Aaron, that they looked
toward the tabernacle of the congregation: and, behold,
the cloud covered it, and the glory of the Lord appeared
[Num. 16:41–42].**

The next day, after they had brooded over it all night, they charge
Moses and Aaron with murdering the rebels! Moses and Aaron didn't
do it, you see; God did it. Notice again that after their murmuring, the
glory of the Lord appears.

Now God is ready to judge this murmuring people. The very man
about whom they are complaining is the one who stands between the
people and God in order to avert His judgment from them.

And the Lord spake unto Moses, saying,

**Get you up from among this congregation, that I may
consume them as in a moment. And they fell upon their
faces.**

**And Moses said unto Aaron, Take a censer, and put fire
therein from off the altar, and put on incense, and go
quickly unto the congregation, and make an atonement**

for them: for there is wrath gone out from the LORD; the plague is begun.

And Aaron took as Moses commanded, and ran into the midst of the congregation; and, behold, the plague was begun among the people: and he put on incense, and made an atonement for the people.

And he stood between the dead and the living; and the plague was stayed.

Now they that died in the plague were fourteen thousand and seven hundred, beside them that died about the matter of Korah.

And Aaron returned unto Moses unto the door of the tabernacle of the congregation: and the plague was stayed [Num. 16:44–50].

The man they rebelled against is the very man who saved them. He stood between them and God. Likewise, the very One whom the human family crucified on the Cross is the One who saves us. He stands between God and the sinner.

CHAPTER 17

THEME: Office of Aaron is attested by resurrection

Now God is going to confirm the priesthood of Aaron and establish the fact that he is the high priest. He will establish this by resurrection!

OFFICE OF AARON IS ATTESTED
BY RESURRECTION

And the Lord spake unto Moses, saying,

Speak unto the children of Israel, and take of every one of them a rod according to the house of their fathers, of all their princes according to the house of their fathers twelve rods: write thou every man's name upon his rod.

And thou shalt write Aaron's name upon the rod of Levi: for one rod shall be for the head of the house of their fathers.

And thou shalt lay them up in the tabernacle of the congregation before the testimony, where I will meet with you.

And it shall come to pass, that the man's rod, whom I shall choose, shall blossom: and I will make to cease from me the murmurings of the children of Israel, whereby they murmur against you [Num. 17:1–5].

The children of Israel were murmuring against Aaron saying that he was not the only one who could represent them before God. It was a rebellion against him.

> And Moses spake unto the children of Israel, and every
> one of their princes gave him a rod apiece, for each
> prince one, according to their fathers' houses, even
> twelve rods: and the rod of Aaron was among their
> rods.
>
> And Moses laid up the rods before the LORD in the taber-
> nacle of witness [Num. 17:6-7].

Now God confirms his priesthood in a most remarkable manner. God
had the prince of each of the twelve tribes bring a rod. These rods
were picked up out on the desert—probably whittled out and deco-
rated by carvings—but they were dead wood. Then these rods were
placed before the Lord in the tabernacle. Aaron's rod was there among
the others, and his rod was as dead as all the others. But what happened?

> And it came to pass, that on the morrow Moses went into
> the tabernacle of witness; and, behold, the rod of Aaron
> for the house of Levi was budded, and brought forth
> buds, and bloomed blossoms, and yielded almonds
> [Num. 17:8].

This is life out of death. Aaron's priesthood was confirmed by resurrection. Aaron's rod brought forth buds, and blossoms, and fruit! Life
out of death. Resurrection. In the springtime the blooming of plants
which have been dormant all winter does not illustrate life out of
death. Neither does the egg. There is a germ of life in the egg. The
perfect illustration of the resurrection of Christ is Aaron's rod that
budded.

The priesthood of the Lord Jesus Christ rests upon the fact of His
resurrection. We are told very frankly in the seventh chapter of Hebrews that if He were here on earth, He would not be a priest. He did
not come from the priestly tribe of Levi. His resurrection made Him a
priest. Then it tells us that not every man becomes a priest. "And no

man taketh this honour unto himself, but he that is called of God, as was Aaron" (Heb. 5:4). Aaron was God's called priest. The evidence was the budded rod—the resurrection.

The Lord Jesus Christ was raised from the dead and He became our High Priest. He has an unchangeable priesthood and so ". . . he is able also to save them to the uttermost that come unto God by him, seeing he ever liveth to make intercession for them" (Heb. 7:25).

At this very moment, He is at God's right hand. He is there for you and for me today. One of the greatest privileges we have is being able to go to Him. He is our Great High Priest who makes intercession for us. "Seeing then that we have a great high priest, that is passed into the heavens, Jesus the Son of God, let us hold fast our profession. For we have not an high priest which cannot be touched with the feeling of our infirmities; but was in all points tempted like as we are, yet without sin. Let us therefore come boldly unto the throne of grace, that we may obtain mercy, and find grace to help in time of need" (Heb. 4:14–16).

Friend, do you need mercy? Do you need help today? Is life monotonous? Is it stale, flat, and unprofitable? Then go to the Lord Jesus. He is up there for you, your Great High Priest. Are you lonely? Go to Him. Is life a battle that you are losing? Are you defeated? Go to Him. Is life a struggle against temptation that you cannot overcome? Go to Him. Is life a horrible mistake and you need wisdom at the crossroads of decision? Go to Him. Is life shrouded with sorrow for you today? Go to Him. He is our Great High Priest by His resurrection from the dead. He is alive! He is up there for us today!

> **And Moses brought out all the rods from before the Lord unto all the children of Israel: and they looked, and took every man his rod.**
>
> **And the Lord said unto Moses, Bring Aaron's rod again before the testimony, to be kept for a token against the rebels; and thou shalt quite take away their murmurings from me, that they die not [Num. 17:9–10].**

Aaron's rod that budded and blossomed and brought forth almonds is to be kept for a testimony and for a token. This rod was one of the three items which were kept in the ark of the covenant: ". . . the ark of the covenant overlaid round about with gold, wherein was the golden pot that had manna, and Aaron's rod that budded, and the tables of the covenant" (Heb. 9:4). The tables of stone on which were written the Ten Commandments, a pot of manna, and the rod that budded were preserved inside the ark of the covenant in the tabernacle. The rod forever settled the question as to the priesthood of Aaron.

CHAPTER 18

THEME: Aaron and the Levites confirmed in their position and responsibilities

We have seen the rebellion of Korah and the 250 princes of Israel against the constituted authority of Moses and Aaron. God judged him and his followers with a very severe judgment because his rebellion was actually against God. Then there were repercussions throughout the camp and a murmuring of the people. They felt the judgment had been too harsh. After all, these had been attractive men, leaders in Israel. Because these soft-hearted folk had no spiritual discernment, they found fault with Moses. Well, Moses was no more guilty of their death than Simon Peter was guilty of the death of Ananias and Sapphira. I'm of the opinion that Moses himself was quite surprised at what really took place.

Then a plague came upon the people because of their murmuring. Aaron stood between the living and the dead, and he became, actually, their intercessor at that time. Then God testified to the priesthood of Aaron by resurrection—He caused Aaron's rod to bud, blossom, and bear fruit. Now God finds it necessary to confirm the priesthood.

AARON AND THE LEVITES CONFIRMED

And the LORD said unto Aaron, Thou and thy sons and thy father's house with thee shall bear the iniquity of the sanctuary: and thou and thy sons with thee shall bear the iniquity of your priesthood [Num. 18:1].

God is telling the Levites that they are responsible for what takes place. We need to remember that Korah was a Levite; the rebellion arose within the tribe of Levi. It was very serious. God is telling them they are responsible.

You and I are responsible today for our Christian testimony, for our families, and for our church. A great many people like to pull their skirts around them and assume a holier-than-thou attitude, shine up their halo, and then look down at the church today and talk about it going into apostasy. Now that is true; the church is going into apostasy. But it is also true that when there is sin in the church, you and I bear a certain amount of responsibility. We cannot escape the responsibility for sin in our lives, sin in our families, and sin in our church.

You see, this is the thing God is saying to Aaron. Aaron cannot look at all that is happening among the Levites and take a holier-than-thou attitude. Aaron cannot elevate himself by pointing that he is God's elect, the one whom God has chosen as the high priest. God's man is to walk in humility. God's man bears responsibility!

> **And thy brethren also of the tribe of Levi, the tribe of thy father, bring thou with thee, that they may be joined unto thee, and minister unto thee: but thou and thy sons with thee shall minister before the tabernacle of witness.**

> **And they shall keep thy charge, and the charge of all the tabernacle: only they shall not come nigh the vessels of the sanctuary and the altar, that neither they, nor ye also, die [Num. 18:2–3].**

God outlines for them very specifically that they, that is Aaron and his sons, are in charge of the sanctuary, the vessels of the sanctuary, and the altar.

Then God goes into detail concerning the part of the offerings that belongs to the priesthood. They were to be sustained by their part of the offerings, and the entire "wave offering" was given to the priest. The wave offering was not offered as a burnt sacrifice, but was given to the priests.

> **All the heave offerings of the holy things, which the children of Israel offer unto the LORD, have I given thee,**

**and thy sons and thy daughters with thee, by a statute
for ever: it is a covenant of salt for ever before the Lord
unto thee and to thy seed with thee [Num. 18:19].**

That was the way a covenant was sealed in that day. Salt was regarded
as a necessary ingredient of the daily food and was used in the sacrifices to the Lord. A covenant of salt became a covenant of permanent
obligation.

**And the Lord spake unto Aaron, Thou shalt have no inheritance in their land, neither shalt thou have any part
among them: I am thy part and thine inheritance among
the children of Israel [Num. 18:20].**

Aaron and all the Levites would have no part in the land. They would
not have farms to keep, or vineyards to tend, or olive groves to protect.
God, Himself, was their inheritance.

May I put this in very plain terms for today? The people in the
church are to pay their preacher. You are to pay the one who is bringing you spiritual food. The man who is spending his time doing that
cannot be working on a farm or in a field or in an office. It is a tragic
thing to see that many of God's finest workmen, both here and in the
mission fields, must take a secular job in order to survive. The ministry suffers, and the church suffers. God provides support for the Levites, and He expected the church to support its pastor.

Now I recognize there are problems in looking to the Lord for His
provisions, but it is also a wonderful thing. I have been a minister for
many, many years, and although there have been difficult times
which have tried our faith, it has been quite marvelous to be in this
position. I want to testify how good God is. He has been mighty good
to this poor preacher. That is what David said in the sixteenth Psalm:
"The Lord is the portion of mine inheritance and of my cup: thou
maintainest my lot" (Ps. 16:5). It is a wonderful thing to have God as
your inheritance, and to have Him as your paymaster, and to look to
Him for every need. It is really a glorious position to be in.

The Lord places the Levites in that position. They lived by faith.

> And, behold, I have given the children of Levi all the tenth in Israel for an inheritance, for their service which they serve, even the service of the tabernacle of the congregation.
>
> Neither must the children of Israel henceforth come nigh the tabernacle of the congregation, lest they bear sin, and die.
>
> But the Levites shall do the service of the tabernacle of the congregation, and they shall bear their iniquity: it shall be a statute for ever throughout your generations, that among the children of Israel they have no inheritance [Num. 18:21-23].

They were to serve in the tabernacle of the congregation, and they were to be supported by the tenth in Israel. This meant that the Levites must walk by faith.

Now the question often arises whether preachers, missionaries, and church staff members should give to the church. I find that today a great many feel that they should not. I'd like to say a word in that connection. We are dealing here with rules and regulations in the Mosaic Law. Although you and I do not live under the Mosaic system, I believe it furnishes great principles by which we are to live. They are road maps for us to help us out in these questionable areas.

> And the LORD spake unto Moses, saying,
>
> Thus speak unto the Levites, and say unto them, When ye take of the children of Israel the tithes which I have given you from them for your inheritance, then ye shall offer up an heave offering of it for the LORD, even a tenth part of the tithe [Num. 18:25-26].

God told the Levites that they were to offer a tenth part of what they received. May I say to you, I think that the Christian worker, whoever he is, is to give to the Lord's work also. I think he ought to give to his church and through his church into his church's program. I have always given to missions and I have always encouraged my staff to give. I always had the offering plate passed on the pulpit platform so we might set an example for the congregation in this matter of giving.

We have had some thrilling experiences, by the way. It is our policy to send out books and tapes to missionaries and not to charge them a thing. But do you know that half of them pay for them? We had a missionary from one of the leading faith missions boards who was home on furlough. He was discouraged and felt he was losing his faith, but he started listening to our program. He never missed one, and then he came to our headquarters to get our tapes. We wanted to give him the tapes, but he insisted he was going to pay for them. May I say to you, he had the right principle.

Many of our missionaries simply cannot pay and we are glad to give them our tapes and materials. I have been impressed by the poverty of the missionaries out on the foreign fields I have visited. They have driven me in cars that were like the one-horse shay, ready to fall apart. Often the gas tank would be so nearly empty I would wonder whether we would make it to the airport. It is a shame and a disgrace that we do not pay our missionaries adequately, nor do we give them the proper instruments and tools to carry out their work.

This eighteenth chapter is a very practical chapter. It has a very definite message for us today.

CHAPTER 19

THEME: The offering and ashes of the red heifer

We come now to one of the most interesting offerings. It is called the offering of the red heifer, and it is most unusual.

THE OFFERING AND ASHES OF THE RED HEIFER

And the LORD spake unto Moses and unto Aaron, saying,

This is the ordinance of the law which the LORD hath commanded, saying, Speak unto the children of Israel, that they bring thee a red heifer without spot, wherein is no blemish, and upon which never came yoke [Num. 19:1–2].

This is the first time an offering is to be a female animal.

And ye shall give her unto Eleazar the priest, that he may bring her forth without the camp, and one shall slay her before his face:

And Eleazar the priest shall take of her blood with his finger, and sprinkle of her blood directly before the tabernacle of the congregation seven times:

And one shall burn the heifer in his sight; her skin, and her flesh, and her blood, with her dung, shall he burn:

And the priest shall take cedar wood, and hyssop, and scarlet, and cast it into the midst of the burning of the heifer.

Then the priest shall wash his clothes, and he shall bathe his flesh in water, and afterward he shall come

> into the camp, and the priest shall be unclean until the
> even.
>
> And he that burneth her shall wash his clothes in water,
> and bathe his flesh in water, and shall be unclean until
> the even [Num. 19:3–8].

Now what is the purpose of this?

> And a man that is clean shall gather up the ashes of the
> heifer, and lay them up without the camp in a clean
> place, and it shall be kept for the congregation of the
> children of Israel for a water of separation: it is a purifi-
> cation for sin [Num. 19:9].

How was this to be used?

> And for an unclean person they shall take of the ashes of
> the burnt heifer of purification for sin, and running wa-
> ter shall be put thereto in a vessel:
>
> And a clean person shall take hyssop, and dip it in the
> water, and sprinkle it upon the tent, and upon all the
> vessels, and upon the persons that were there, and upon
> him that touched a bone, or one slain, or one dead, or a
> grave:
>
> And the clean person shall sprinkle upon the unclean
> on the third day, and on the seventh day: and on the sev-
> enth day he shall purify himself, and wash his clothes,
> and bathe himself in water, and shall be clean at even
> [Num. 19:17–19].

This is an unusual ordinance, and it sounds very strange, but there is
a good reason for it. When the children of Israel were on the march
and a man sinned, they couldn't stop right there, put up the tabernacle, and go through the ritual of offering a trespass offering or a sin

offering. So what were they to do when a man sinned on the way? They would take the ashes of this heifer, mix those ashes with running water, then with hyssop sprinkle the individual who had sinned. That sounds very strange, doesn't it? But that was the way God dealt with sin for those people.

Let me tell you another strange incident. When our Lord Jesus Christ went into the Upper Room with His disciples, the first thing He did was to get a basin of water and wash the disciples' feet. Now why did He do that? He tells Simon Peter the reason. ". . . If I wash thee not, thou hast no part with me" (John 13:8). If the Lord Jesus had not washed the feet of Peter, Peter could not have fellowship with Him. He had come from the Father and He was going back to the Father. "Jesus knowing that the Father had given all things into his hands, and that he was come from God, and went to God; He riseth from supper, and laid aside his garments; and took a towel, and girded himself" (John 13:3–4).

Jesus Christ has gone back to the Father now, and He is still girded with the towel of service. The basin of water is the Word of God, the Holy Spirit is the One who applies it, and the hyssop speaks of faith.

When you and I sin today, Christ is not going to die all over again. We are told, "But if we walk in the light, as he is in the light, we have fellowship one with another, and the blood of Jesus Christ his Son cleanseth us from all sin" (1 John 1:7). That "light" is the Word of God. If we walk in the light, what do we see? We see that we are dirty and that we need cleaning. The Spirit of God convicts us. The Word tells us that the blood of Jesus Christ, God's Son, will keep on cleansing us from all these sins. But the water of the Word and the cleansing blood of Jesus Christ must be applied to us. "If we confess our sins, he is faithful and just to forgive us our sins, and to cleanse us from all unrighteousness" (1 John 1:9). He died down here to save us. He lives up yonder to keep us saved. When Jesus Christ died for our sins, He did not die only for those sins up to the time we came to Him. He died for our sins from the time we came to Him at the Cross until He gives us a crown.

Don't tell me that you don't sin after you have been saved. Sin in our lives is a fact which so many Christians neglect. Christian people

get cleaned up for church. They take their Saturday night bath to be
clean for Sunday. Congregations smell better today than they used to
smell because they use deodorants, perfumes and colognes, but to
God they smell worse because they are dirty. How many have been
looking at things they shouldn't look at? They come with dirty eyes.
How many have been listening to gossip during the week? How many
have been hearing filthy things they shouldn't hear? They come with
dirty ears. Some have dirty hands because they have been doing
things they shouldn't have done. Some have dirty feet because they
have been walking where they shouldn't have walked. They think that
coming to church makes everything all right. Well, it's not all right.
That's the reason the Lord Jesus says, ". . . If I wash thee not, thou hast
no part with me" (John 13:8). If the church service seems dead, and
the sermon boring, perhaps it's because you need a bath, a spiritual
bath. "If we say that we have fellowship with him, and walk in darkness, we lie, and do not the truth" (1 John 1:6). We don't want to lie. If
we do, then we have to confess that to Him. It is so important to go to
Him and to tell Him all our sins. And you might just as well tell Him
because He already knows all about you anyway. But it makes fellowship so wonderful if we confess our sins to Him.

Why don't you go to Him for cleansing? Someone may ask how
often this should be done. Well, I don't know about you, but I try to
take a shower every day. And I find that I must go to Him two or three
times every day and tell Him that McGee has been wrong and that
McGee shouldn't have seen this, or done this, or said that. May I say to
you, we want to keep sweet with Him, and the only way we can do
that is to confess our sins.

This offering of the red heifer is a marvelous offering. It kept the
children of Israel sweet on the wilderness march. This was their deo-
dorant for the wilderness march so that they might walk in fellowship
with Him.

CHAPTER 20

THEME: At Kadesh again (after 37 years); the seventh murmuring; water from rock, disobedience of Moses; Edom refuses Israel passage through their land; death of Aaron

The chapter before us opens with the death of Miriam and it closes with the death of Aaron. The chapter is bounded by death. It also contains the sin of Moses and the sin of Edom. Yet this is an important chapter because it marks the end of wandering for the children of Israel and the beginning of marching.

This section, from chapters 14 to 20, is the only section which deals with the forty years of wandering in the wilderness—and that's not very much. We have only a few incidents that took place during these forty years. Israel is out of God's will, and there is little to tell. We can talk about Israel being God's chosen people, but they didn't amount to anything except when they were in God's will. And that is still true today.

It is also true of you and me that we don't amount to anything when we are out of the will of God. When you and I are not functioning in the body of believers, exercising the gift that He has given to us by the power of the Holy Spirit, we are as unnecessary as a fifth leg on a cow. Actually, we get in the way.

AT KADESH AGAIN (AFTER 37 YEARS)

Then came the children of Israel, even the whole congregation, into the desert of Zin in the first month: and the people abode in Kadesh; and Miriam died there, and was buried there [Num. 20:1].

Here we have the death of Miriam and only one verse is given to it. There is no long funeral oration, no days of mourning, no effort to eulogize. Miriam died and was buried. That's all.

They are back at Kadesh. They had been here almost thirty-eight years before and now they're back again. Thirty-eight years of wandering, going nowhere. Although these years of wandering were not years of great blessing for the people, they provide great lessons to be learned because many of us today are not marching as pilgrims through the world; we are simply wandering pilgrims in this world down here.

THE SEVENTH MURMURING

And there was no water for the congregation: and they gathered themselves together against Moses and against Aaron.

And the people chode with Moses, and spake, saying, Would God that we had died when our brethren died before the Lord [Num. 20:2–3].

Of course they don't really mean that. None of us wants to die. Death is unnatural for man. But they are complaining, whining again, and murmuring. This is the seventh murmuring, and it is over the lack of water.

And why have ye brought up the congregation of the Lord into this wilderness, that we and our cattle should die there?

And wherefore have ye made us to come up out of Egypt, to bring us in unto this evil place? it is no place of seed, or of figs, or of vines, or of pomegranates; neither is there any water to drink [Num. 20:4–5].

Here they are back at Kadesh where they had failed before, and again they are complaining instead of trusting. Well, the land of milk and honey is ahead of them, but it isn't here.

I don't care where you are today, or who you are—you as a child of

God need to recognize that you are not here permanently. All of us are just pilgrims passing through this world; we won't be in any one place for long. So we ought not to spend so much time complaining.

> **And Moses and Aaron went from the presence of the assembly unto the door of the tabernacle of the congregation, and they fell upon their faces: and the glory of the LORD appeared unto them [Num. 20:6].**

Again I call your attention to the fact that every time these people murmured or complained, the glory of the Lord appeared. God was displeased with their complaining. That should make us realize that if we are whining and complaining saints, we are not pleasing to God. That is true no matter who you are, or where you are, or what you are doing.

WATER FROM ROCK, DISOBEDIENCE OF MOSES

> **And the LORD spake unto Moses, saying,**

> **Take the rod, and gather thou the assembly together, thou, and Aaron thy brother, and speak ye unto the rock before their eyes; and it shall give forth his water, and thou shalt bring forth to them water out of the rock: so thou shalt give the congregation and their beasts drink [Num. 20:7–8].**

"Take the rod"—this rod was Aaron's, by the way. "Gather the assembly together, and speak unto the rock." Why were they simply to speak to the rock this time? It is because many years before this (as recorded in the seventeenth chapter of Exodus) the rock was smitten and water came forth. The rock is to be smitten only once!

> **And Moses took the rod from before the LORD, as he commanded him.**

**And Moses and Aaron gathered the congregation to-
gether before the rock, and he said unto them, Hear
now, ye rebels; must we fetch you water out of this rock?
[Num. 20:9–10].**

Not only are the children of Israel complaining, but Moses is complaining now, don't you think? I have great sympathy for him. He's
been with them all of forty years in the wilderness, and frankly, he is
getting pretty tired of them.

He is forgetting himself here in verse 11 when he says, "Must we
fetch you water out of this rock?" Moses is not going to fetch them
water out of the rock at all. God is the One who will provide the water.
They need to learn a great lesson here which is that the rock is a type
of Christ. Now Moses became angry and he did something that he
should not have done. This is going to keep him from entering the
Promised Land.

**And Moses lifted up his hand, and with his rod he
smote the rock twice: and the water came out abundantly, and the congregation drank, and their beasts
also [Num. 20:11].**

Some men teach that his error was in smiting the rock twice. He
should not have smitten it at all, friend. It had already been smitten.
The rock is a type of Christ (1 Cor. 10:4). Christ suffered once for sins,
never the second time. He died once. God was teaching this to them in
a type, and Moses should have protected and guarded the type by
obeying God. God told him very clearly that he was to speak to the
rock. That was all he needed to do. But Moses failed to obey God. The
importance of this act of disobedience was that the rock pictures
Christ. "Moreover, brethren, I would not that ye should be ignorant,
how that all our fathers were under the cloud, and all passed through
the sea; And were all baptized unto Moses in the cloud and in the sea;
And did all eat the same spiritual meat; And did all drink the same
spiritual drink: for they drank of that spiritual Rock that followed
them: and that Rock was Christ" (1 Cor. 10:1–4).

The water came out abundantly. The error of Moses did not keep the water from coming out. How gracious God is!

And the LORD spake unto Moses and Aaron, Because ye believed me not, to sanctify me in the eyes of the children of Israel, therefore ye shall not bring this congregation into the land which I have given them [Num. 20:12].

God is saying here that Moses and Aaron did not believe Him, neither did they sanctify Him in the eyes of Israel. That is, they took to themselves the credit for the miracle.

When we read the New Testament, we find that Moses did reach the Promised Land eventually; he appeared on the Mount of Transfiguration with Christ in that land.

Canaan is actually the picture of where you and I should live by faith. It is not a picture of heaven. We are in this world which is a wilderness, but you and I ought to be enjoying the blessings of Canaan. That comes, as we shall see in the book of Joshua, by the death and resurrection of Christ. We are to reckon upon that, believing God and yielding to Him in this matter. That is what Moses and Aaron failed to do.

This is the water of Meribah; because the children of Israel strove with the LORD, and he was sanctified in them [Num. 20:13].

Today, unbelief is our great sin also. My, what a reflection it is on God when we don't take Him at His Word and believe Him!

EDOM REFUSES ISRAEL PASSAGE THROUGH THEIR LAND

And Moses sent messengers from Kadesh unto the king of Edom, Thus saith thy brother Israel, Thou knowest all the travail that hath befallen us:

> How our fathers went down into Egypt, and we have
> dwelt in Egypt a long time; and the Egyptians vexed us,
> and our fathers:
>
> Let us pass, I pray thee, through thy country: we will
> not pass through the fields, or through the vineyards,
> neither will we drink of the water of the wells: we will
> not turn to the right hand nor to the left, until we have
> passed thy borders [Num. 20:14–15, 17].

Moses gives them a little history of their nation, and then he asks for permission to cross their land. Now that was a request that was made in a very kind sort of way. Edom was their brother, and Moses reminds them of this. Edom sinned by not letting them pass through.

> And Edom said unto him, Thou shalt not pass by me,
> lest I come out against thee with the sword [Num.
> 20:18].

The children of Israel again told Edom that they had their cattle and little ones and wanted to come through. Again they assured them that they would not take anything or damage the land.

> And he said, Thou shalt not go through. And Edom
> came out against him with much people, and with a
> strong hand.
>
> Thus Edom refused to give Israel passage through his
> border: wherefore Israel turned away from him.
>
> And the children of Israel, even the whole congregation,
> journeyed from Kadesh, and came unto mount Hor
> [Num. 20:20–22].

Now they are making a circuitous route which would not have been necessary had they been given permission to go through Edom. However, I think that Moses made a mistake here. Moses should have been following the cloud. He didn't need to worry. God would be leading him and guiding him. Instead of asking Edom for permission to go through, he should have simply followed the cloud. I think that the pillar of cloud would have led him in a way so he would never have had to fight Edom at all. I believe this is a case of running ahead of the Lord. Unfortunately, many of us do that.

DEATH OF AARON

We come now to the death of Aaron and that brings us to the end of the chapter which ends on a sad note. But there are very precious lessons in this chapter for you and for me.

> **And the Lord spake unto Moses and Aaron in mount Hor, by the coast of the land of Edom, saying,**

> **Aaron shall be gathered unto his people: for he shall not enter into the land which I have given unto the children of Israel, because ye rebelled against my word at the water of Meribah [Num. 20:23–24].**

You know, there are many people today who are saved, but even in this life they never enjoy the fruits of salvation and they do not have the peace of the Spirit in their own lives. They do not know what it is to walk in fellowship with the Lord Jesus. Yet I would never for one moment question their salvation. Aaron was typical of that kind of life. He knew forty years of rugged experience in the wilderness, but he never knew what it was to sit down and enjoy the fruits of the Promised Land. He did not know what it was to drink the milk and eat the honey in the land of milk and honey. Many of us rob ourselves of that because of our unbelief.

> **Take Aaron and Eleazar his son, and bring them up unto mount Hor:**

And strip Aaron of his garments, and put them upon
Eleazar his son: and Aaron shall be gathered unto his
people, and shall die there.

And Moses did as the Lord commanded: and they went
up into mount Hor in the sight of all the congregation.

And Moses stripped Aaron of his garments, and put
them upon Eleazar his son; and Aaron died there in the
top of the mount: and Moses and Eleazar came down
from the mount.

And when all the congregation saw that Aaron was
dead, they mourned for Aaron thirty days, even all the
house of Israel [Num. 20:25–29].

There is a precious lesson here for us. This was a very sad thing in
Israel, but it has in it for us today something that should cause us to
thank God.

The children of Israel mourned for thirty days. I think there were
many in that company who had been to Aaron, the high priest. They
knew Aaron, and Aaron knew them. They would bring their sacrifice
and they would ask Aaron, "Oh, do you think God will forgive me?"
And I think that Aaron would comfort them and tell them that our
God is a gracious, merciful God. Then he would offer their sacrifice
for them. Now they saw Eleazar come down clothed in the garments of
Aaron. Aaron is dead and gone. And they would say, "I don't know
Eleazar and he doesn't know me. It's a different priest now."

May I say to you today that we have a High Priest who ever lives to
make intercession for us. Our Lord is not a Priest after the order of
Aaron but after the order of Melchizedek. He has neither beginning of
days, nor end of life; He abides a Priest continually! Our High Priest
will not die. He died once for us down here; He lives forever for us up
there. He will always be there for us. We can always depend on Him.
He knows each of us individually and we can know Him. To know
Him is life everlasting. Knowing Him will occupy us for all eternity

and it will never be changed. That is something to be thankful for today.

Israel has finished the wilderness wandering now and will be getting ready to enter into the Promised Land. Also God has a "promised land" into which He wants to bring us today. Christ is the One who can bring us there right now.

CHAPTER 21

THEME: Victory of Israel; the eighth murmuring; the serpent of brass; first song; the march of Israel

As we have seen, chapter 20 brought us to the end of the wilderness wanderings in the sense that the wandering is over and they begin to march. In this chapter are their first victories in warfare. Also the experience of their eighth and last murmuring is recorded, which brought about the fiery serpents and the serpent of brass, used by the Lord Jesus to illustrate His own crucifixion.

VICTORY OF ISRAEL

And when king Arad the Canaanite, which dwelt in the south, heard tell that Israel came by the way of the spies; then he fought against Israel, and took some of them prisoners.

And Israel vowed a vow unto the LORD, and said, If thou wilt indeed deliver this people into my hand, then I will utterly destroy their cities.

And the LORD hearkened to the voice of Israel, and delivered up the Canaanites; and they utterly destroyed them and their cities: and he called the name of the place Hormah.

And they journeyed from mount Hor by the way of the Red sea, to compass the land of Edom: and the soul of the people was much discouraged because of the way [Num. 21:1-4].

This is the first victory (since their conflict with Amalek shortly after they left Egypt) on the wilderness march. God clearly gave them this victory. However they now have to go by Mount Hor by way of the Red

Sea. Since they can't go through the land of Edom, they are attempting to make a circuitous route around that land. The way is hard and
becomes very discouraging to the people. In their plight of discouragement, they begin to complain and whine and murmur. Unfortunately this is characteristic of many of us today. When life is hard we
complain and murmur.

THE EIGHTH MURMURING

**And the people spake against God, and against Moses.
Wherefore have ye brought us up out of Egypt to die in
the wilderness? for there is no bread, neither is there any
water; and our soul loatheth this light bread [Num.
21:5].**

This is the eighth and last murmuring of the children of Israel. They
are murmuring again about the manna. You will recall that the mixed
multitude were the ones who had led them in rejecting the manna
earlier in the march. Manna was a wonderful food, by the way. God
reminds them in the Book of Deuteronomy that their feet did not
swell. A missionary doctor in the Philippines told me that the foot
will swell and beriberi results from a diet deficiency. So they were
getting all the correct nutrition in the manna, and it was a very tasty
sort of food. Yet they complained.

There are people who will complain about steak—they would
want a hamburger for variety! It's amazing how easy it is for us to
complain, and especially to complain about that which pertains to the
things of God. When I was a pastor, people complained about the
seats in the church. Yet I've seen folk go to a football game and sit on
hard seats in a stadium (and there is no back on those seats) for hours
and never complain! Now I will admit that when they listened to me
preach they noticed the seats more. But isn't it interesting how we
whine and complain to God? How many times do we thank Him and
rejoice in His goodness to us?

I think, frankly, that the Lord is getting just a little tired of all their
murmuring. They say that their soul hates this manna. They don't

want it. They charge God with bringing them into this wilderness to die. The Lord is tired of all their complaining and He is going to judge them for it.

THE SERPENT OF BRASS

And the LORD sent fiery serpents among the people, and they bit the people; and much people of Israel died.

Therefore the people came to Moses, and said, We have sinned, for we have spoken against the LORD, and against thee; pray unto the LORD, that he take away the serpents from us. And Moses prayed for the people [Num. 21:6–7].

"We have sinned." They are now ready to admit that they have sinned against the Lord and against Moses.

Now, that is a problem with many folk today. They want to begin with God as a church member, as a nice little girl or boy. We all must begin with God as sinners. The only way that God will begin with us is as sinners. You see, Christ died for sinners, and He loves sinners. If you can't come in under that category, then Christ is not for you. He came for sinners.

These people are going to have to give evidence of faith because they have no good works. They can't come to God with the promise that from now on they will be good because they won't be good. But they can believe God, and God is going to let them come to Him by faith.

And the LORD said unto Moses, Make thee a fiery serpent, and set it upon a pole: and it shall come to pass, that every one that is bitten, when he looketh upon it, shall live.

And Moses made a serpent of brass, and put it upon a pole, and it came to pass, that if a serpent had bitten any

**man, when he beheld the serpent of brass, he lived
[Num. 21:8-9].**

There is a marvelous lesson here, you see. They are to look at the brazen serpent, and they are to look in faith. In fact, they would not look
if it were not in faith. I can well imagine some of the folk saying that
this was just nonsense. They would want something else, something
more tangible than just turning around to look at a serpent of brass.
But, of course, if a man would not turn to look at the serpent of brass,
he would die.

Now, we don't have to guess at the meaning of this and the lesson
for us. When our Lord was talking to Nicodemus on that dark night,
He said, "And as Moses lifted up the serpent in the wilderness, even
so must the Son of man be lifted up: That whosoever believeth in him
should not perish, but have eternal life. For God so loved the world,
that he gave his only begotten Son, that whosoever believeth in him
should not perish, but have everlasting life" (John 3:14-16).

How was the Son of man lifted up? You say, on a cross. Yes, but He
was dying on the cross of Barabbas, and Barabbas was a thief and a
murderer. Barabbas was guilty and was worthy of death. Jesus was
not. Our Lord was made sin for us. On that cross, He not only has
taken the place of Barabbas but also your place and my place. God
permitted this and did this because He loves us. But God cannot save
us by His love. It doesn't say that God so loved the world that He saved
the world. Not at all. God so loved the world that He *gave* His only
begotten Son. Now what God asks you to do, my friend, is to look and
live. Look to Christ! He is taking your place there. You are a sinner and
it is you who deserves to die. Christ did not deserve to die. He died for
you.

We read here that this serpent of brass was made, and those who
looked to it lived. Those who did not look to it—died. It is just that
simple today. Either you are looking to Christ as your Savior because
you are a sinner, or you are not doing it. If you are not doing it, I don't
care how many times you have been baptized, how many ceremonies
you have been through, how many churches you have joined, or who

your father and mother happened to be, you are a lost, hell-doomed sinner. You must look to the Lord Jesus Christ. It is just as simple as that. And by the way, it is just as complicated as that. What a problem people have today. They would rather look to themselves and to their own good works, trusting that somehow their own good works might save them. It is a problem for people to admit they are sinners and to look to Christ and trust Him.

Now the children of Israel move on. They come to the River Arnon which you can trace on your map.

> From thence they removed, and pitched on the other side of Arnon, which is in the wilderness that cometh out of the coasts of the Amorites: for Arnon is the border of Moab, between Moab and the Amorites [Num. 21:13].

Then they go on.

> And from thence they went to Beer: that is the well whereof the LORD spake unto Moses, Gather the people together, and I will give them water [Num. 21:16].

FIRST SONG

Now listen to this. How different this is. This is the first time they sing a song of praise and thanksgiving. They have been singing the desert blues and murmuring. Now it's the Hallelujah chorus.

> Then Israel sang this song, Spring up, O well; sing ye unto it:

> The princes digged the well, the nobles of the people digged it, by the direction of the lawgiver, with their staves. And from the wilderness they went to Mattanah:

> And from Mattanah to Nahaliel: and from Nahaliel to Bamoth:

> And from Bamoth in the valley, that is in the country of
> Moab, to the top of Pisgah, which looketh toward Jeshi-
> mon [Num. 21:17-20].

They were thanking God for the provision that He had made for them
in supplying water. The princes digged the well and the nobles of the
people digged. Here you find capital and labor joining together in
this.

THE MARCH OF ISRAEL

> And Israel sent messengers unto Sihon king of the Amo-
> rites, saying [Num. 21:21].

Israel now asks Sihon, king of the Amorites, for permission to pass
through his land. Sihon refuses and gathers an army against Israel.

> And Israel smote him with the edge of the sword, and
> possessed his land from Arnon unto Jabbok, even unto
> the children of Ammon: for the border of the children of
> Ammon was strong [Num. 21:24].

God gave Israel the victory over Sihon.

> And they turned and went up by the way of Bashan: and
> Og the king of Bashan went out against them, he, and
> all his people, to the battle of Edrei [Num. 21:33].

The Lord told Moses not to fear Og, the king of Bashan. They smote
him and his sons and his people and they possessed the land of
Bashan.

The children of Israel are marching now. They are singing praises
to God and God is giving them victory. God will help them against
Moab, too. They will then be getting ready to enter the Promised
Land.

CHAPTER 22

THEME: The way of Balaam

Chapters 22 to 25 comprise a section of Numbers which goes into the story of Balaam, the prophet. He comes across the page of Scripture as one of those strange individuals whom I wish I could interpret for you. I wish I knew more so that I could correctly evaluate him.

There are literally thousands of people recorded in the Word of God. The Holy Spirit customarily gives us a cameo-sharp picture of them, a clear delineation of their character in just a few words. We've seen that.

Then there are the exceptions—these few walk in the shadows. Darkness hides their true natures. They are distorted, twisted individuals. I am not sure about Cain, or about Esau, Samson, or Saul, Absalom, or this man Balaam. I am not sure how to interpret them. Then in the New Testament we have questions about that rich, young ruler who came to Christ. Did he ever come back to Christ? Then there is Judas. Who can understand him? I'm sure that most of us feel that he was a lost individual, but he's a strange person who followed our Lord for three years. No one detected that he was a phony except the Lord Jesus Himself. Then there is Demas—Demas who seemed to be so faithful and yet who finally forsook the apostle Paul. And what about Ananias and Sapphira?

Balaam is one of those enigmatic and mysterious characters. One writer says that he is the strangest of all characters in the Scripture. Some authors consider him a genuine prophet of God. Others say he was a religious racketeer. Is Balaam sincerely seeking to serve God, or is he a fake, a phony? Well, I'll have to let you be the judge of that.

We might say that we should dismiss him as unworthy of any consideration, but I must tell you that the Word of God attaches some importance to him. Micah writes, "Oh my people, remember now what Balak king of Moab consulted, and what Balaam the son of Beor answered him from Shittim unto Gilgal; that ye may know the righteousness of the LORD" (Mic. 6:5). Micah is telling Israel that they had better not forget him. So we had better not push this character aside.

Did you know that there is more said in Scripture about Balaam than there is about Mary, the mother of Jesus? There is more said about Balaam than about any of the apostles. The New Testament mentions him three times, and each time it is in connection with apostasy. In 2 Peter we are told about the *way* of Balaam. In Revelation we are told about the *doctrine* of Balaam.

This Balaam was a Midianite. He was a prophet with a wide reputation. He got results. Was he genuine? Let's read his story before we evaluate him.

THE WAY OF BALAAM

And the children of Israel set forward, and pitched in the plains of Moab on this side Jordan by Jericho.

And Balak the son of Zippor saw all that Israel had done to the Amorites.

And Moab was sore afraid of the people, because they were many: and Moab was distressed because of the children of Israel [Num. 22:1–3].

You see that Israel is ready to enter the land. Balak, king of the Moabites, had witnessed what had happened to the Amorites and to Og, the king of Bashan. He was wondering what he should do to get Israel out of the land. Should he attack them? Very candidly, he didn't know what to do. So he decided to engage the services of this prophet.

He sent messengers therefore unto Balaam the son of Beor to Pethor, which is by the river of the land of the children of his people, to call him, saying, Behold, there is a people come out from Egypt: behold, they cover the face of the earth, and they abide over against me:

> Come now therefore, I pray thee, curse me this people;
> for they are too mighty for me: peradventure I shall pre-
> vail, that we may smite them, and that I may drive them
> out of the land: for I wot that he whom thou blessest is
> blessed, and he whom thou cursest is cursed [Num.
> 22:5-6].

He sends for Balaam. Apparently this prophet was well known in that entire land. Balak wants to hire him to come and curse the children of Israel. These people had poured into the area there by the Jordan River and Balak wanted them out of that land.

> And the elders of Moab and the elders of Midian de-
> parted with the rewards of divination in their hand; and
> they came unto Balaam, and spake unto him the words
> of Balak [Num. 22:7].

He sent messengers down to Balaam to make this overture to him. The man has quite a reputation, you see. The messengers bring their rewards, or the pay, for the diviner. Balaam is a fortune teller. Balak offers a very handsome price to this man through his messengers.

> And he said unto them, Lodge here this night, and I will
> bring you word again, as the LORD shall speak unto me:
> and the princes of Moab abode with Balaam [Num.
> 22:8].

Now he seems honestly to be trying to ascertain here the mind of God. He apparently is in touch with God. Now notice:

> And God came unto Balaam, and said, What men are
> these with thee?
>
> And Balaam said unto God, Balak the son of Zippor,
> king of Moab, hath sent unto me, saying,

> Behold, there is a people come out of Egypt, which cov-
> ereth the face of the earth: come now, curse me them;
> peradventure I shall be able to overcome them, and
> drive them out [Num. 22:9-11].

It is a very interesting thing that God did communicate with him.

> And God said unto Balaam, Thou shalt not go with
> them; thou shalt not curse the people: for they are
> blessed [Num. 22:12].

Now that was a categorical, matter-of-fact answer. There was no way
to be evasive about that. Now watch Balaam.

> And Balaam rose up in the morning, and said unto the
> princes of Balak, Get you into your land: for the LORD
> refuseth to give me leave to go with you [Num. 22:13].

Balaam seems to be a sincere and honest man of God. If this were the
end of the story, then I would have to assume that about him, but Balak was a persistent fellow.

> And Balak sent yet again princes, more, and more hon-
> ourable than they.

> And they came to Balaam, and said to him, Thus saith
> Balak the son of Zippor, Let nothing, I pray thee, hinder
> thee from coming unto me:

> For I will promote thee unto very great honour, and I
> will do whatsoever thou sayest unto me: come therefore,
> I pray thee, curse me this people [Num. 22:15-17].

Actually, you see, they are offering a better price.

> And Balaam answered and said unto the servants of Ba-
> lak, If Balak would give me his house full of silver and

> gold, I cannot go beyond the word of the LORD my God,
> to do less or more [Num. 22:18].

Well, they had upped the price but that does not seem to affect this man Balaam. He turns it down. He sounds very pious here. I feel like saying Amen. Then I have a second thought. He's too good to be true. Just why did he speak of a house filled with silver and gold? He said it because that is what he is thinking about. He is covetous, and his mind is turned in that direction.

> Now therefore, I pray you, tarry ye also here this night,
> that I may know what the LORD will say unto me more
> [Num. 22:19].

Oh, oh, what is happening here, friends? Well, it's quite obvious. He already has an answer from God. He has no need to wait another night for a further answer from God. God had already told him not to go, but you see, this man is hoping that the Lord will open a little crack in the door so he can put his foot into it; and if he can get his foot into it, then he is going to go. This is all very interesting.

Do we sometimes do this same thing? We who are preachers make a great deal about a call from God. I heard the story of a preacher who came home and told his wife one day, "Honey, I just had a call to the church over in the next town. Now you know it's a bigger town, richer town, bigger church, more members, and fine folk over there. I've been called to go over there as pastor and I'm going upstairs to pray about it and find out what the Lord's will is for us." She answered, "I'll go upstairs to pray with you." "Oh no," he said, "you stay down here and pack!" He had made up his mind, as you can see. Old Balaam had made up his mind also.

Now notice what happens. God does not do this for Balaam only; He does it for you and for me. It is not good, friends, but God permits us to do what we want to do.

> And God came unto Balaam at night, and said unto
> him, If the men come to call thee, rise up, and go with

> them; but yet the word which I shall say unto thee, that
> shalt thou do [Num. 22:20].

In other words, God is saying, "All right, you want to go and before it is through you will go, but if you go, you are to say what I want you to say. Be careful of that." We have here what is known as the permissive will of God. He permits us many times to do something that we insist on doing when it is not in His direct will. You remember how we learned from the children of Israel that God granted their request but sent leanness to their souls. Sometimes He also grants our requests and sends leanness to our souls.

> And Balaam rose up in the morning, and saddled his
> ass, and went with the princes of Moab.
>
> And God's anger was kindled because he went: and the
> angel of the LORD stood in the way for an adversary
> against him. Now he was riding upon his ass, and his
> two servants were with him.
>
> And the ass saw the angel of the LORD standing in the
> way, and his sword drawn in his hand: and the ass
> turned aside out of the way, and went into the field: and
> Balaam smote the ass, to turn her into the way [Num.
> 22:21-23].

He had God's direct answer, but he didn't like that. God permits him to go. Now God sends His angel, but this prophet doesn't have the mind of God at all. We can see that he has no spiritual discernment, not even the discernment of this dumb animal.

> But the angel of the LORD stood in a path of the vine-
> yards, a wall being on this side, and a wall on that side.
>
> And when the ass saw the angel of the LORD, she thrust
> herself unto the wall, and crushed Balaam's foot
> against the wall: and he smote her again.

> And the angel of the LORD went further, and stood in a narrow place, where was no way to turn either to the right hand or to the left [Num. 22:24-26].

Balaam was determined to go, you see. He was a covetous man.

> And when the ass saw the angel of the LORD, she fell down under Balaam: and Balaam's anger was kindled, and he smote the ass with a staff.
>
> And the LORD opened the mouth of the ass, and she said unto Balaam, What have I done unto thee, that thou hast smitten me these three times? [Num. 22:27-28].

This is a miracle, of course. God is using this method to get His message through.

A wag once said that it was a miracle in Balaam's day when an ass spoke, and it's a miracle in our day when one keeps quiet! That's probably true.

> And Balaam said unto the ass, Because thou hast mocked me: I would there were a sword in mine hand, for now would I kill thee.
>
> And the ass said unto Balaam, Am not I thine ass, upon which thou hast ridden ever since I was thine unto this day? was I ever wont to do so unto thee? And he said, Nay.
>
> Then the LORD opened the eyes of Balaam, and he saw the angel of the LORD standing in the way, and his sword drawn in his hand: and he bowed down his head, and fell flat on his face [Num. 22:29-31].

The angel warned Balaam again that he was to speak only the word which the Lord would tell him. So Balaam went on to his meeting with the king, Balak.

> And the angel of the LORD said unto him, Wherefore hast thou smitten thine ass these three times? behold, I went out to withstand thee, because thy way is perverse before me:
>
> And the ass saw me, and turned from me these three times: unless she had turned from me, surely now also I had slain thee, and saved her alive.
>
> And Balaam said unto the angel of the LORD, I have sinned; for I knew not that thou stoodest in the way against me: now therefore, if it displease thee, I will get me back again.
>
> And the angel of the LORD said unto Balaam, Go with the men: but only the word that I shall speak unto thee, that thou shalt speak. So Balaam went with the princes of Balak [Num. 22:32–35].

This is what Scripture calls the *way* of Balaam. Speaking of false prophets, Peter wrote, "Which have forsaken the right way, and are gone astray, following the way of Balaam the son of Bosor, who loved the wages of unrighteousness; But was rebuked for his iniquity: the dumb ass speaking with man's voice forbad the madness of the prophet" (2 Pet. 2:15–16). The *way* of Balaam was covetousness.

Unfortunately, this is the way that a great many Christians and Christian organizations are measured today—by the dollar sign. May God keep you and me from the sin of covetousness!

Now notice the scene here. Balaam goes on his way and arrives at the location where Israel is encamped.

> And when Balak heard that Balaam was come, he went out to meet him unto a city of Moab, which is in the border of Arnon, which is in the utmost coast.
>
> And Balak said unto Balaam, Did I not earnestly send unto thee to call thee? wherefore camest thou not unto me? am I not able indeed to promote thee to honour?

And Balaam said unto Balak, Lo, I am come unto thee: have I now any power at all to say any thing? the word that God putteth in my mouth, that shall I speak.

And Balaam went with Balak, and they came unto Kirjath-huzoth.

And Balak offered oxen and sheep, and sent to Balaam, and to the princes that were with him.

And it came to pass on the morrow, that Balak took Balaam, and brought him up into the high places of Baal, that thence he might see the utmost part of the people [Num. 22:36–41].

Balak, the king of Moab, takes him to the top of a mountain where he can see the camp of Israel below.

CHAPTER 23

THEME: The first prophecy; the second prophecy; the error of Balaam

Here we see "the error of Balaam"—ignorance of God's righteousness. This is an impressive scene. Balaam has now come to Balak, the king of Moab. Balak takes Balaam to the top of a mountain so that he can see the camp of Israel below. The fact of the matter is that Balak is not satisfied with any of the prophecies of Balaam; so he will take him to four different mountains on four different sides of the camp.

THE FIRST PROPHECY

Balak took Balaam up into the high places of Baal. There they offered burnt offerings, and there the Lord put a word into Balaam's mouth.

> And he took up his parable, and said, Balak the king of Moab hath brought me from Aram, out of the mountains of the east, saying, Come, curse me Jacob, and come, defy Israel.

> How shall I curse, whom God hath not cursed? Or how shall I defy, whom the LORD hath not defied?

> For from the top of the rocks I see him, and from the hills I behold him: lo, the people shall dwell alone, and shall not be reckoned among the nations.

> Who can count the dust of Jacob, and the number of the fourth part of Israel? Let me die the death of the righteous, and let my last end be like his!

> And Balak said unto Balaam, What hast thou done unto me? I took thee to curse mine enemies, and behold, thou hast blessed them altogether.

> And he answered and said, Must I not take heed to
> speak that which the LORD hath put in my mouth?
> [Num. 23:7–12].

Here is the first of the remarkable prophecies concerning the people of
Israel. This wasn't at all what Balak wanted him to say. He wasn't
satisfied with this prophecy; so he took Balaam over to another mountain to give him another look at the children of Israel as they were
camped in the valley.

THE SECOND PROPHECY

Balak took Balaam to the top of Pisgah and there they offered burnt
offerings. They could see Israel down in the camp, and again the Lord
met Balaam and put a word in his mouth.

> And he took up his parable, and said, Rise up, Balak,
> and hear; hearken unto me, thou son of Zippor:
>
> God is not a man, that he should lie; neither the son of
> man, that he should repent: hath he said, and shall he
> not do it? Or hath he spoken, and shall he not make it
> good?
>
> Behold, I have received commandment to bless: and he
> hath blessed; and I cannot reverse it.
>
> He hath not beheld iniquity in Jacob, neither hath he
> seen perverseness in Israel: the LORD his God is with
> him, and the shout of a king is among them.
>
> God brought them out of Egypt; he hath as it were the
> strength of an unicorn.
>
> Surely there is no enchantment against Jacob, neither is
> there any divination against Israel: according to this
> time it shall be said of Jacob and of Israel, What hath
> God wrought!

> Behold, the people shall rise up as a great lion, and lift
> up himself as a young lion: he shall not lie down until he
> eat of the prey, and drink the blood of the slain [Num.
> 23:18-24].

Instead of cursing Israel, he actually blesses them again. God makes it
very clear that he is not to curse Israel.

THE ERROR OF BALAAM

Now we see what Balaam is doing. He uses his own reasoning and
rationalizing, and concludes that God must condemn Israel. There
was evil in the camp. Sin was in evidence. They failed miserably. We
have just seen the incident of the brazen serpent, and the people there
confessed that they had sinned. So Balaam came to this natural conclusion: God must judge Israel because of their sins.

The natural man always concludes that God must judge Israel because of their sin, and that God must judge the individual sinner. So
many times I hear a question like this: "How could God call David a
man after His own heart?" Well, there is a higher righteousness than
human righteousness, and that is the righteousness of Christ. "What
shall we then say to these things? If God be for us, who can be against
us? He that spared not his own Son, but delivered him up for us all,
how shall he not with him also freely give us all things? Who shall lay
any thing to the charge of God's elect? It is God that justifieth. Who is
he that condemneth? It is Christ that died, yea rather, that is risen
again, who is even at the right hand of God, who also maketh intercession for us" (Rom. 8:31-34).

God does not judge the sinner because He has already judged him
in Christ Jesus—when he came to God by faith in Christ. The world
does not understand that. Old Balaam didn't understand that. He
thought that God must condemn Israel. He figured that if God was
going to judge Israel, he might as well get the benefit of the rewards
from King Balak. He thought that God would condemn Israel and that
he would be permitted to get a handsome reward as a result of it.

Balaam did not understand the righteousness of God. He did not understand that the believing sinner, just like the people of Israel, could not come under the judgment and condemnation of God. When the believer sins, he comes under the disciplining hand of God, not under the condemnation of God.

Again Balak is not satisfied. He takes Balaam to the top of Peor for another view of Israel.

CHAPTER 24

The story of Balaam continues uninterruptedly from the previous chapter.

THE THIRD PROPHECY

And when Balaam saw that it pleased the Lord to bless Israel, he went not, as at other times, to seek for enchantments, but he set his face toward the wilderness.

And Balaam lifted up his eyes, and he saw Israel abiding in his tents according to their tribes; and the spirit of God came upon him [Num. 24:1–2].

Here is something which leaves us in amazement. The Spirit of God came upon this man. Listen to his prophecy.

And he took up his parable, and said, Balaam the son of Beor hath said, and the man whose eyes are open hath said:

He hath said, which heard the words of God, which saw the vision of the Almighty, falling into a trance, but having his eyes open:

How goodly are thy tents, O Jacob, and thy tabernacles, O Israel!

As the valleys are they spread forth, as gardens by the river's side, as the trees of lign aloes which the Lord hath planted, and as cedar trees beside the waters.

He shall pour the water out of his buckets, and his seed
shall be in many waters, and his king shall be higher
than Agag, and his kingdom shall be exalted.

God brought him forth out of Egypt; he hath as it were
the strength of an unicorn: he shall eat up the nations
his enemies, and shall break their bones, and pierce
them through with his arrows.

He couched, he lay down as a lion, and as a great lion:
who shall stir him up? Blessed is he that blesseth thee,
and cursed is he that curseth thee [Num. 24:3-9].

There was sin in the camp of Israel, but God had dealt with that. He
had set up the brazen serpent. The sins had been forgiven. God is not
going to permit anyone on the outside to bring a charge against them.
All that Balaam can do is to bless them and to praise them.

Just so, Satan cannot bring a charge against God's elect. "Who
shall lay any thing to the charge of God's elect? It is God that justifieth. Who is he that condemneth? It is Christ that died, yea rather,
that is risen again, who is even at the right hand of God, who also
maketh intercession for us" (Rom. 8:33-34). "What shall we then say
to these things? If God be for us, who can be against us?" (Rom. 8:31).
I haven't anything to say but hallelujah! Who can make a charge
against God's elect? No one. God has already declared them righteous.

And Balak's anger was kindled against Balaam, and he
smote his hands together: and Balak said unto Balaam,
I called thee to curse mine enemies, and behold, thou
hast altogether blessed them these three times.

Therefore now flee thou to thy place: I thought to pro-
mote thee unto great honour: but, lo, the LORD hath kept
thee back from honour.

And Balaam said unto Balak, Spake I not also to thy
messengers which thou sentest unto me, saying,

> If Balak would give me his house full of silver and gold,
> I cannot go beyond the commandment of the LORD, to do
> either good or bad of mine own mind; but what the LORD
> saith, that will I speak?
>
> And now, behold, I go unto my people: come therefore,
> and I will advertise thee what this people shall do to thy
> people in the latter days [Num. 24:10–14].

Of course Balak is angry, but Balaam reminds him that he cannot
prophesy anything beyond the commandment of the Lord.

THE FOURTH PROPHECY

> And he took up his parable, and said, Balaam the son of
> Beor hath said, and the man whose eyes are open hath
> said:
>
> He hath said, which heard the words of God, and knew
> the knowledge of the most High, which saw the vision of
> the Almighty, falling into a trance, but having his eyes
> open [Num. 24:15–16].

Notice this carefully. It is a most remarkable prophecy, and this is
one we hear at Christmas time.

> I shall see him, but not now: I shall behold him, but not
> nigh: there shall come a Star out of Jacob, and a Sceptre
> shall rise out of Israel, and shall smite the corners of
> Moab, and destroy all the children of Sheth.
>
> And Edom shall be a possession, Seir also shall be a
> possession for his enemies; and Israel shall do valiantly.
>
> Out of Jacob shall come he that shall have dominion,
> and shall destroy him that remaineth of the city [Num.
> 24:17–19].

Have you ever stopped to wonder where the wise men learned to look
for a star? How did they associate a star with a king born over in Israel? Why would they make such a long trek?

About 1500 years after this prophecy was given, we find coming
out of the east, the land of Balaam, a whole company of wise men.
Apparently this prophecy of Balaam was retained, since Balaam was
considered an outstanding prophet in the east, and the wise men
knew his prophecy. When they saw the remarkable star, they remembered that Balaam had said, ". . . there shall come a Star out of Jacob,
and a Sceptre shall rise out of Israel . . ." (Num. 25:17). When the wise
men came to Jerusalem, their question was, "Where is he that is born
King of the Jews? for we have seen his star in the east, and are come to
worship him?" (Matt. 2:2). When we add to these Scriptures the
prophecy of Daniel (and Daniel likewise had prophesied in the east)
which gives the approximate time that the Messiah would come, we
see that the coming of the wise men to Jerusalem is very understand-
able.

The thing that makes it very remarkable is that Israel, the people
who had the Old Testament with all the prophecies of Christ's coming,
was not looking for Him—with the exception of a very small minority,
such as Anna and Simeon. When this company of wise men (there
were probably nearer three hundred than three!) converged on Jerusalem, the entire city, including Herod the king, was stirred. Their coming adds a thrilling dimension to the Christmas story. And it is quite
interesting to trace it to this old rascal, Balaam.

Now Balaam prophesied concerning the nations around Israel.

> **And when he looked on Amalek, he took up his para-
> ble, and said, Amalek was the first of the nations; but
> his latter end shall be that he perish for ever.**

> **And he looked on the Kenites, and took up his parable,
> and said, Strong is thy dwellingplace, and thou puttest
> thy nest in a rock.**

> **Nevertheless the Kenite shall be wasted, until Asshur
> shall carry thee away captive.**

And he took up his parable, and said, Alas, who shall live when God doeth this!

And ships shall come from the coast of Chittim, and shall afflict Asshur, and shall afflict Eber, and he also shall perish for ever [Num. 24:20–24].

He certainly didn't satisfy King Balak with his prophecies.

And Balaam rose up, and went and returned to his place: and Balak also went his way [Num. 24:25].

That is a very strange statement concerning Balaam. He rose up and went and returned to his place. There is only one other man in Scripture who is said to have gone to his place and that man is Judas (Acts 1:25). The Scriptures are pretty silent about that.

We learn in Numbers 31:8 that Balaam was killed in battle along with the kings of Midian. ". . . Balaam also the son of Beor they slew with the sword." Balaam was slain and, like Judas, he went to his place.

CHAPTER 25

THEME: The doctrine of Balaam—fornication with the
Moabites and embracing their idolatry

In this chapter we shall see the most subtle and satanic thing which
this man Balaam really did. We have discovered the *way* of Balaam
(2 Pet. 2:15) which is the way of covetousness. He was after the almighty dollar, and he was willing to sacrifice his principles for that.
Then, in Jude 11, we read of the error of Balaam. His error was that he
was not aware of the fact that God could declare righteous those sin- ·
ners who trust in Him. Now we see in Revelation the doctrine of Balaam, the damnable thing which this man taught. "But I have a few
things against thee, because thou hast there them that hold the doctrine of Balaam, who taught Balac to cast a stumblingblock before the
children of Israel, to eat things sacrificed unto idols, and to commit
fornication" (Rev. 2:14). When Balaam saw that he could not curse
Israel, he taught Balak how he might corrupt these people. We hear
this same idea today. "If you can't lick 'em, join 'em." Because Balak
couldn't fight these people, Balaam taught him to join them and corrupt them from within.

THE DOCTRINE OF BALAAM

And Israel abode in Shittim, and the people began to
commit whoredom with the daughters of Moab.

And they called the people unto the sacrifices of their
gods: and the people did eat, and bowed down to their
gods.

And Israel joined himself unto Baal-peor: and the anger
of the LORD was kindled against Israel [Num. 25:1–3].

Do you see what happened? Balaam couldn't curse Israel, but he could tell Balak what to do. They should infiltrate Israel, integrate with them, intermarry with them, and introduce idolatry to them to turn them away from their God.

I'm sure they told Israel not to be a bunch of squares, not to be so narrow-minded. They insisted they were broad-minded and invited Israel to come over and worship with them. But they never went to worship with the children of Israel.

It has always interested me that a liberal in the church wants me, a fundamentalist, to come over on his side and agree with him. But I have never been able to get him to come over to my side and agree with me—yet he claims to be the broad-minded fellow and I am the narrow-minded fellow. It is very interesting that the tendency of the human heart is always downward and away from God. This is the reason religious rackets prosper—TV and radio religious rackets, church religious rackets, and educational religious rackets. Look how the people support such things. They appeal to the natural man. This is the reason some of those people think I am pretty foolish to teach the Bible. If I introduced something other than the Word of God, the program would prosper. I am very sorry to have to tell you that that is the way it is. Old Balaam knew that Balak could corrupt the people by getting a religious racket going. He could appeal to them and get the children of Israel to turn to the worship of Baal. And that is exactly what happened.

> **And the Lord said unto Moses, Take all the heads of the people, and hang them up before the Lord against the sun, that the fierce anger of the Lord may be turned away from Israel.**

> **And Moses said unto the judges of Israel, Slay ye every one of his men that were joined unto Baal-peor [Num. 25:4–5].**

You say that is extreme surgery. It certainly is. And do you know why? Because the disease is fatal! This would turn a man away from God and send him to hell; therefore, God is performing an act of mercy to save the nation Israel.

> And, behold, one of the children of Israel came and brought unto his brethren a Midianitish woman in the sight of Moses, and in the sight of all the congregation of the children of Israel, who were weeping before the door of the tabernacle of the congregation.
>
> And when Phinehas, the son of Eleazar, the son of Aaron the priest, saw it, he rose up from among the congregation, and took a javelin in his hand;
>
> And he went after the man of Israel into the tent, and thrust both of them through, the man of Israel, and the woman through her belly. So the plague was stayed from the children of Israel.
>
> And those that died in the plague were twenty and four thousand [Num. 25:6-9].

You see, this was the way that Balaam was able to curse Israel. This is the doctrine of Balaam.

Our Lord tells us in Revelation that that same doctrine gets into the church, and is in the church today. My viewpoint is that the enemy can't hurt God's people or God's work or God's church from the outside. The church has never been hurt from the outside. To the church at Pergamos our Lord said, "But I have a few things against thee, because thou hast there them that hold the doctrine of Balaam, who taught Balac to cast a stumblingblock before the children of Israel, to eat things sacrificed unto idols, and to commit fornication" (Rev. 2:14). This is the doctrine of Balaam. In the history of the early church, Pergamos marked the union of the world and the church. The world came in like a flood, and the Devil joined the church at Pergamos. It was not persecution from the outside, but the doctrine of Balaam on the inside that hurt the church.

This great principle is applicable in all relationships of life.

After World War II, we stationed missiles everywhere. We did everything to keep the enemy outside. What happened? We began to fall from the inside. There began a moral decay such as we had never before seen in our country. Today we find the revolutionaries are on the inside of our nation. We are being destroyed from within. Rome didn't fall from the outside. No enemy from the outside destroyed Rome, but Rome fell from within.

Have you ever noticed that the Lord Jesus was betrayed from the inside? It wasn't a Roman soldier who betrayed Him. It was one of His own apostles who betrayed Him over to Rome to be crucified. Jesus is always betrayed from the inside. That is still true today. That is the doctrine of Balaam and it is a damnable doctrine.

Now the covenant of the priesthood is given to Phinehas, the son of Eleazar, the son of Aaron the priest. And the Lord tells Moses to vex the Midianites and smite them. And that closes this chapter.

And the Lord spake unto Moses, saying,

Phinehas, the son of Eleazar, the son of Aaron the priest, hath turned my wrath away from the children of Israel, while he was zealous for my sake among them, that I consumed not the children of Israel in my jealousy.

Wherefore say, Behold, I give unto him my covenant of peace:

And he shall have it, and his seed after him, even the covenant of an everlasting priesthood; because he was zealous for his God, and made an atonement for the children of Israel.

Now the name of the Israelite that was slain, even that was slain with the Midianitish woman, was Zimri, the son of Salu, a prince of a chief house among the Simeonites.

And the name of the Midianitish woman that was slain was Cozbi, the daughter of Zur; he was head over a people, and of a chief house in Midian.

And the LORD spake unto Moses, saying,

Vex the Midianites, and smite them:

For they vex you with their wiles, wherewith they have beguiled you in the matter of Peor, and in the matter of Cozbi, the daughter of a prince of Midian, their sister, which was slain in the day of the plague for Peor's sake [Num. 25:10–18].

CHAPTER 26

THEME: Census of the new generation

This is the beginning of a new section of the Book of Numbers. The new generation is preparing to enter the land. The remainder of the Book of Numbers is occupied with this preparation.

CENSUS OF THE NEW GENERATION

When we compare the census taken the second year of their wilderness march with the census taken the fortieth year of their march, we find a considerable difference. The following chart, prepared by Keil and Delitzsch in their *Commentary on the Old Testament* shows that while there was considerable increase in some of the tribes, there was a decided decrease in others. The total decrease for Israel was 1,820.

	First Numbering	Second Numbering
Reuben	46,500	43,730
Simeon	59,300	22,200
Gad	45,650	40,500
Judah	74,600	76,500
Issachar	54,400	64,300
Zebulon	57,400	60,500
Ephraim	40,500	32,500
Manasseh	32,200	52,700
Benjamin	35,400	45,600
Dan	62,700	64,400
Asher	41,500	53,400
Naphtali	53,400	45,400
Total	603,550	601,730

For example, the tribe of Reuben became smaller by 2,770 persons.

> These are the families of the Reubenites: and they that
> were numbered of them were forty and three thousand
> and seven hundred and thirty [Num. 26:7].

If you turn back to the census in the first chapter, you will find,
"Those that were numbered of them, even of the tribe of Reuben, were
forty and six thousand and five hundred" (Num. 1:21). That was forty
years earlier when they started out in the wilderness.

In contrast to Reuben, the tribe of Dan showed a marked increase.

> These are the sons of Dan after their families: of Shu-
> ham, the family of the Shuhamites. These are the fami-
> lies of Dan after their families.
>
> All the families of the Shuhamites, according to those
> that were numbered of them, were threescore and four
> thousand and four hundred [Num. 26:42–43].

At the first census it was said of Dan, "Those that were numbered of
them, even of the tribe of Dan, were threescore and two thousand and
seven hundred" (Num. 1:39). In other words, Dan increased by 1,700
persons.

However, the second census revealed that Israel was smaller by
1,820 persons. The old generation died in the wilderness, just as God
had told them. "Your carcases shall fall in this wilderness; and all that
were numbered of you, according to your whole number, from twenty
years old and upward, which have murmured against me" (Num.
14:29).

> But among these there was not a man of them whom
> Moses and Aaron the priest numbered, when they num-
> bered the children of Israel in the wilderness of Sinai.
>
> For the LORD had said of them, They shall surely die in
> the wilderness. And there was not left a man of them,
> save Caleb the son of Jephunneh, and Joshua the son of
> Nun [Num. 26:64–65].

This is now the new generation. All the old generation, except Caleb and Joshua, have died. God did not hold those who were under twenty responsible for the failure and rebellion at Kadesh-barnea. This may give us some indication as to the age of accountability. I do not know when it is, and I do not mean to suggest that it is twenty, but I think it is older than many of us suspect.

This is a new generation with the exception of two men. We are going to get better acquainted with these two interesting men when we come to the book of Joshua.

CHAPTER 27

THEME: The women's problem; God grants their request; Moses is to prepare for death

We are in the section of the Book of Numbers which we have labeled "A New Generation." We saw last time that when the census was made, Joshua and Caleb were the only persons living who were enlisted in the census the first time. In other words, every one twenty years and over had died in that forty-year period. Those were rigorous years out on that desert, and they had perished. Now Israel is comprised of a new generation, and this new generation will have new problems.

It has always been a problem for one generation to understand another generation because each generation faces its own particular problem. It is quite interesting that someone has divided it this way. When you are young, you criticize the old generation, and when you are old, you criticize the young generation. That seems to be human nature.

As we come to this twenty-seventh chapter of the Book of Numbers we see that the new generation is presented here with a new problem. Actually, Moses didn't know what to do. He had to appeal to the Lord, because according to the laws of other nations the women just didn't count. In fact, they were treated as chattel.

THE WOMEN'S PROBLEM

Then came the daughters of Zelophehad, the son of Hepher, the son of Gilead, the son of Machir, the son of Manasseh, of the families of Manasseh the son of Joseph: and these are the names of his daughters; Mahlah, Noah, and Hoglah, and Milcah, and Tirzah [Num. 27:1].

If you have a lot of daughters in your family, friends, and you run out names, and you don't like ordinary names, here is a list I'd like to suggest to you: Mahlah, Noah, Hoglah, Milcah, and Tirzah! I have never heard of a woman named any of these names, and I think I know why! But these were the daughters of Zelophehad.

> **And they stood before Moses, and before Eleazar the priest, and before the princes and all the congregation, by the door of the tabernacle of the congregation, saying,**
>
> **Our father died in the wilderness, and he was not in the company of them that gathered themselves together against the LORD in the company of Korah; but died in his own sin, and had no sons.**
>
> **Why should the name of our father be done away from among his family, because he hath no son? Give unto us therefore a possession among the brethren of our father.**
>
> **And Moses brought their cause before the LORD [Num. 27:2–5].**

You can see the problem. This man Zelophehad died in the wilderness. He had five daughters and no sons. According to the Mosaic Law, it looked as if a son were the one who inherited the property, and the women were just left out. Certainly the laws of the other nations did leave them out. They did not count at all. Now what are they to do?

These daughters of Zelophehad are very aggressive. We are hearing a great deal today about women's rights. Well, they certainly got their rights in the Bible. There are those who said years ago that the Bible was a man's book. However the more I read the Bible, the more I see that the Word of God gives women their rights. And I believe that they should have their rights, by the way.

Moses didn't really know what to do. I suppose he said to them,

"Well, girls, I don't know what to say to you. I can see that you have a just cause, but according to the laws and customs of the day you certainly would not get anything." So Moses brought their case before the Lord.

GOD GRANTS THEIR REQUEST

And the LORD spake unto Moses, saying,

The daughters of Zelophehad speak right: thou shalt surely give them a possession of an inheritance among their father's brethren; and thou shalt cause the inheritance of their father to pass unto them [Num. 27:6–7].

The Lord is on the side of women's rights, you see. This is one of the most remarkable laws that is imaginable. We live in a day when a ruling such as this is commonplace. It is difficult for us to put ourselves back in that day when women were treated like chattel. Missionaries who work among the tribes on the Orinoco River were telling me recently that in Venezuela a little girl in the family is sold to a man even before she reaches the age of ten years. Girls are traded just as one would trade an animal. This custom still exists among primitive people. Every woman today ought to be thankful for the Word of God because it is the Bible that first gave women their rights. I think this is a marvelous thing. "The daughters of Zelophehad speak right: thou shalt surely give them a possession of an inheritance." Now, on the basis of that, God puts down a principle and a law for them.

And thou shalt speak unto the children of Israel, saying, If a man die, and have no son, then ye shall cause his inheritance to pass unto his daughter.

And if he have no daughter, then ye shall give his inheritance unto his brethren.

And if he have no brethren, then ye shall give his inheritance unto his father's brethren.

And if his father have no brethren, then ye shall give his inheritance unto his kinsman that is next to him of his family, and he shall possess it: and it shall be unto the children of Israel a statute of judgment, as the LORD commanded Moses [Num. 27:8-11].

This is a marvelous step forward, and it was made about 1500 years before Christ came into the world. I marvel at the aggressiveness and the forwardness of these women. I marvel at the faith of these women. "But without faith it is impossible to please him: for he that cometh to God must believe that he is, and that he is a rewarder of them that diligently seek him" (Heb. 11:6). The five girls wanted to possess their father's inheritance. It was not the custom of the day nor a written law that they could have it. Therefore, they asked by faith, and by faith God gave the inheritance to them.

There is a marvelous lesson in this for us today. We are told that we are blessed with all spiritual blessings in heavenly places in Christ (Eph. 1:3). I believe that God hears and answers us, not only in the spiritual blessings but also in the material things. I'm of the opinion that most of us are more or less paupers because we do not come to God as his children and ask Him for things. God wants to be good to us.

In my Christian life I have always hesitated to ask God for any material thing. When I was attending seminary, I worked for a Memphis newspaper, taking in ads at night. When there was an ad to sell a car, I'd go out and look at the car. If it was a bargain, I would buy it. I would drive it a year or so, then sell it for what I had paid for it. When I graduated from seminary, I asked the Lord to give me a good second-hand car. Do you know what the Lord did? He gave me a new car. Now, why didn't I ask Him for a new car? Perhaps we are poor because we just don't know what to ask for.

More than this, we have possessions—wonderful spiritual possessions in Christ Jesus. He would like for us to claim these in faith. The daughters of Zelophehad came and asked for the possession that was their father's. Today we have spiritual possessions which we should

ask for. Let's tell our Father that we want our inheritance and that we
want these spiritual blessings. He wants to bless us! How wonderful
He is!

MOSES IS TO PREPARE FOR DEATH

We come to a sad note here. We've been following Moses for a long
time. Actually, because he is the writer of Genesis, we have been with
him from Genesis until now. At this point he is to prepare to pass from
this earthly scene

> And the LORD said unto Moses, Get thee up into this
> mount Abarim, and see the land which I have given
> unto the children of Israel.
>
> And when thou hast seen it, thou also shalt be gathered
> unto thy people, as Aaron thy brother was gathered.
>
> For ye rebelled against my commandment in the desert
> of Zin, in the strife of the congregation, to sanctify me at
> the water before their eyes: that is the water of Meribah
> in Kadesh in the wilderness of Zin [Num. 27:12–14].

God is referring to the time Moses smote that rock twice after God had
told him to speak to it. God says here that it was rebellion against His
commandment. Because Moses did this, he is only permitted to take a
look into the land; he is not permitted to enter the land.

I used to ask my classes a trick question. Did Moses ever enter the
Promised Land? Most of the students would say that he did not. Every
now and then a sharp student would say, "Yes, he did." And, of
course, he did. He was there on the Mount of Transfiguration with the
Lord Jesus. That was after his death.

Here he only got a view of the Promised Land. God will not permit
him to enter into the land. You see, disobedience keeps many of us
from entering into our spiritual possessions. Disbelief will always
lead to disobedience. That is exactly what happened to Moses.

And Moses spake unto the Lord, saying,

Let the Lord, the God of the spirits of all flesh, set a man over the congregation,

Which may go out before them, and which may go in before them, and which may lead them out, and which may bring them in; that the congregation of the Lord be not as sheep which have no shepherd.

And the Lord said unto Moses, Take thee Joshua the son of Nun, a man in whom is the spirit, and lay thine hand upon him;

And set him before Eleazar the priest, and before all the congregation; and give him a charge in their sight [Num. 27:15–19].

There is to be a successor appointed to take the place of Moses. He must be a Spirit-filled man. Now I want to make it clear that the laying on of hands did not make him Spirit-filled, nor did it give him any power. The only thing that can be communicated by the laying on of hands is disease germs. What it does indicate is succession or partnership in the enterprise. You will remember that the church put their hands on Paul and Barnabas and sent them out from Antioch. Did that give them power? Not at all. The power came through the Holy Spirit of God. It was to show that the church was acknowledging their association with these two men in the missionary enterprise. That is the meaning of the laying on of hands.

Joshua is to be the successor of Moses. After Moses lays down the work, Joshua will pick it up. We will learn a great deal about this man when we get to the Book of Joshua. I want to say here that I think Joshua was the most surprised man in the camp when he was chosen to succeed Moses. In one sense he was the most unlikely one to succeed Moses. Do you know why? He was an average man. No one went around saying that Joshua had great potential, great leadership ability, and all that sort of thing you hear today. Apparently Joshua didn't have that. He was an ordinary individual. Joshua reveals what God can do with an ordinary man.

I must tell you that the Books of Joshua and Judges have always been a great encouragement to me. I love those two books because they reveal what God can do with ordinary men. If a person will be yielded to Him, God can take him and use him. That means He can use me, because He can use the ordinary. It means He can use you.

So Joshua is the chosen one. He is appointed to take the place of Moses. We will see that in due time, after the death of Moses at the end of the Book of Deuteronomy, Joshua takes over.

> **And Moses did as the LORD commanded him: and he took Joshua, and set him before Eleazar the priest, and before all the congregation:**
>
> **And he laid his hands upon him, and gave him a charge, as the Lord commanded by the hand of Moses [Num. 27:22–23].**

CHAPTERS 28 AND 29

THEME: Law of the offerings

Now that Israel is prepared to enter the Promised Land by a new census which mustered the able-bodied men for warfare, and by the appointment of Joshua as commander, its spiritual life is dealt with. The offerings have already been instituted, but here, for the sake of completeness, all the national sacrifices which were to be offered during the whole year are reviewed.

Because in Leviticus we looked at these offerings in detail, we will only touch on certain points here that are particularly interesting and meaningful.

Why did God spend so much time with the details of these offerings? Very candidly, it is rather tedious. This is especially true in our day when we do not offer bloody sacrifices. And it must have been tedious for them also. I marvel at how meticulous things had to be for the offering unto God. Why is there such detail? The reason is so wonderful that I wouldn't want you to miss it for anything in the world. It is actually the preciousness of Christ that is brought to our attention here—in fact, the abiding preciousness of Christ.

LAW OF THE OFFERINGS

And the LORD spake unto Moses, saying,

Command the children of Israel, and say unto them, My offering, and my bread for my sacrifices made by fire, for a sweet savour unto me, shall ye observe to offer unto me in their due season [Num. 28:1–2].

Notice the emphasis—"*My* offering . . . *my* bread . . . *my* sacrifice . . . unto *me*." You recall from the Book of Leviticus that there were two kinds of offerings. Of the five offerings, three of them were sweet savor offerings; two of them were non-sweet savor offerings. The sweet savor offerings represented the person of Christ; the non-sweet offerings speak of the work of Christ in redemption for you and me. Now here God is talking about sweet savor offerings, and He calls them My offerings. These offerings represent not what Christ has done for us, or our thoughts of Him, but they speak of what God thinks of Him.

Now what does this mean to you and me? We hear a lot today about worship and worship services. But how much is true worship in our services? How much is just aimless activity? Real worship is when we think God's thoughts after Him. This sweet savor offering which God speaks of as My offering, My bread, My sacrifice, represents what God thinks of Christ. God is satisfied with what Christ did for you and me on the cross. What about you? Are you satisfied with what Christ did for you on the cross? Are you resting in that today? His invitation is "Come unto me, all ye that labour and are heavy laden, and I will give you rest" (Matt. 11:28). Have you brought your burden of sin to Him and received Him as your Savior? Are you satisfied with who He is? If He is not the Son of God, then what He did is absolutely meaningless. True worship is a recognition of who He is and an adoration of His Person. In other words, it is thinking God's thoughts after Him.

> **And thou shalt say unto them, This is the offering made by fire which ye shall offer unto the LORD: two lambs of the first year without spot day by day, for a continual burnt offering [Num. 28:3].**

That burnt offering, speaking of the Person of Christ, all went up in smoke; it all ascended to God. And this is the aspect of this sacrifice that is all important.

When we come to chapter 29, we find it is a continuation of the laws of the offerings.

God wanted His people to come to Him with joy on these wonderful, high, holy days, the feast days. The exception was the Day of Atonement.

And ye shall have on the tenth day of this seventh month an holy convocation; and ye shall afflict your souls: ye shall not do any work therein [Num. 29:7].

This was a repetition of the law as given in Leviticus. "Also on the tenth day of this seventh month there shall be a day of atonement: it shall be an holy convocation unto you; and ye shall afflict your souls, and offer an offering made by fire unto the LORD" (Lev. 23:27).

This chapter concludes with the law of offerings for the Feast of Tabernacles. Offerings for their sins and trespasses are mentioned, but always this is given in addition to the burnt offerings.

There are marvelous lessons for us in these two chapters. Friend, you and I are sinners. Even if you didn't know it, you are a sinner. If you and I pay close attention to the Word of God, we will find that we are sinners and need a Savior. We need Christ! We need a Savior who died for us and paid the penalty for our sins.

Sin is what has brought sorrow into this world. Sin has brought the tears and the broken heart. God hates sin. I'm glad He hates sin. God is moving forward today—undeviatingly, unhesitatingly, uncompromisingly—against sin. He intends to drive it out of His universe. God will not compromise with it at all. He will not accept the white flag of truce. He intends to eliminate it, and I'm thankful for that.

Because it is sin that has robbed you and me of our fellowship with Him, sin is an occasion for mourning. When was the last time you wept over your sins? Have you been before God, my friend, and wept over your sin, over the failure of your life, over your coldness and indifference? My, how we need to confess that to Him today. It is not because God is high and we are low, or because He is great and we are small, nor because He is infinite and we are finite that we are separated from Him. He says it is our sins that have separated us from Him. That is the occasion for weeping.

Let me be very frank with you. I was ordained into the ministry in 1933, and was an active pastor for thirty-seven years. I have had successful pastorates, as man judges those things. There has always been an increase in attendance, and a new interest in Bible study, thriving and growing young people's work, and people being saved. You may ask, "Isn't that a cause of rejoicing?" I confess to you that I don't rejoice. I look back and I see my failure, and I see it in a very glaring way. Don't misunderstand—I'm not guilty of shooting anybody or of committing adultery, but I failed my Savior in so many ways, so many times, and I confess that to Him. I let things come in to separate me in times when I needed His fellowship and wanted His fellowship. But I'd let these things come in the way. That is occasion for mourning, even for weeping to this day.

But God did not want His people to spend a life of mourning. There was only one day of mourning. All the others were feasts of joy. These were the sin offerings and the trespass offerings. Christ has atoned for our sins on the cross. How we needed that! But the emphasis is on the burnt offerings, the burnt offering continually every day and the burnt offerings of the feast days. God is delighted in His Son.

All of the details speak of our Savior and how wonderful He is. He is a sweet savor offering; that is who He is. He is the non-sweet savor offering; that is what He did. He was made sin for us, He who knew no sin. I am the sinner, but He died in my stead so that I might be made the righteousness of God in Him. He took my place down here and He has given me His place up there. If you are saved today, you have as much right in heaven as Christ has. Did you know that? You have *His* right to be there, and if you don't have His right, then you have no business there—in fact, you *won't* be there. We are accepted in the Beloved. That is the basis on which God receives us. If you are in Him, you just can't improve on that at all. How wonderful this is.

CHAPTER 30

THEME: A vow is inviolate: a woman's vow depends upon her father or husband; the vow of a widow or divorced woman must stand

A fter the law of the offerings, we have the law of the vows. The law of the vows in this chapter has special reference to women. We have seen that women have been given the right to claim their inheritance. Now we learn that women also have responsibility.

A VOW IS INVIOLATE

We had a whole chapter on vows in Leviticus and there we called attention to the importance which God attaches to vows. He warns His children that they should be careful if they are making a vow to God. God will hold a person to his vow; so the warning is not to make a vow foolishly.

I think there is a grave danger today for people to promise the Lord too much. As I neared the end of my ministry, I became very reluctant to ask people to take any kind of vow before God, except to accept Christ as Savior. Why? Because I've seen multitudes come to an altar to dedicate their lives and then I've seen those people break their vows. God doesn't ask us to make vows—they are voluntary—but if we make a vow, God means business with us, and He will hold us to our vow.

> And Moses spake unto the heads of the tribes concerning the children of Israel, saying, This is the thing which the LORD hath commanded.
>
> If a man vow a vow unto the LORD, or swear an oath to bind his soul with a bond; he shall not break his word, he shall do according to all that proceedeth out of his mouth [Num. 30:1-2].

This is very important for Christians today. Paul has this in mind when he says, ". . . if thou shalt confess with thy mouth the Lord Jesus, and shalt believe in thine heart that God hath raised him from the dead, thou shalt be saved. For with the heart man believeth unto righteousness; and with the mouth confession is made unto salvation" (Rom. 10:9–10). How do you believe on the Lord Jesus Christ? With your heart. And then what happens? Confession is made by your mouth. Confessing with your mouth is your vow, that is your statement of faith. The point of it is not just what the mouth says, but that the heart must believe what the mouth is saying. These two must be in agreement. "For with the heart man believeth unto righteousness." You don't believe with your mouth, you *say* it with the mouth. "And with the mouth confession is made unto salvation." The heart and the mouth must be singing the same tune, in a duet together. That is exactly what is meant in this matter of vows.

A WOMAN'S VOW DEPENDS UPON
HER FATHER OR HUSBAND

If a woman also vow a vow unto the LORD, and bind herself by a bond, being in her father's house in her youth;

And her father hear her vow, and her bond wherewith she hath bound her soul, and her father shall hold his peace at her: then all her vows shall stand, and every bond wherewith she hath bound her soul shall stand [Num. 30:3–4].

In other words, if a woman makes a vow while she is still single and in her father's home, the father can be held responsible for her. If the father keeps quiet when he hears her make the vow, then that vow which she made will stand. However, if the father speaks up and says, "Wait just a minute. She has bought this dress, and I don't intend to pay for it," then he is protected in the matter. That vow is not binding.

> But if her father disallow here in the day that he heareth;
> not any of her vows, or of her bonds wherewith she hath
> bound her soul, shall stand: and the LORD shall forgive
> her, because her father disallowed her [Num. 30:5].

Now what happens if the woman is married?

> And if she had at all an husband, when she vowed, or
> uttered ought out of her lips, wherewith she bound her
> soul;
>
> And her husband heard it, and held his peace at her in
> the day that he heard it: then her vows shall stand, and
> her bonds wherewith she bound her soul shall stand.
>
> But if her husband disallowed her on the day that he
> heard it; then he shall make her vow which she vowed,
> and that which she uttered with her lips, wherewith she
> bound her soul, of none effect: and the LORD shall for-
> give her [Num. 30:6–8].

If the married woman goes out and makes expensive purchases and
obligates herself, the husband can say that he disallows it and will not
be responsible to pay for it. The vow will not stand and he is not obli-
gated. So you see that either a father or a husband could be held responsible for the vow a woman made, unless they had disallowed it.

Sometimes we see this principle bypassed today. There are women
who are gold-diggers. They marry a man for his money. One sees this
at times when a younger woman marries an older man. After she has
his name, she can go to court and get practically everything that he
owns. I've seen that happen several times. I knew a Christian man
who was lonely after the death of his wife, and who then married a
young woman who was really after the money. This man had willed
his money to mission boards and Christian organizations, but the
young widow was able to break the will and get the money for herself
so that the Christian organizations got none of it. Also I have had men

tell me about marrying women who have taken them for everything they had. Well, that's the foolishness of mankind. God says a man does not need to permit this sort of thing.

THE VOW OF A WIDOW OR
DIVORCED WOMAN MUST STAND

But every vow of a widow, and of her that is divorced, wherewith they have bound their souls, shall stand against her [Num. 30:9].

A widow must stand on her own two feet. The vow that she makes stands. You notice how important these details are to God. He wants His people always to be as good as their word.

God keeps His vows, and He expects His children to keep theirs. He made a vow to Abraham. He made a promise to David. God will stand behind His vows. He has kept His promises in the past and will keep His promises in the future. "For God so loved the world, that he gave his only begotten Son, that whosoever believeth in him should not perish, but have everlasting life" (John 3:16). That is the Word of God, God's promise to you and me. And the Word of God stands. He has vowed that He will save you if you trust in Christ, and that vow stands. A dear, little Scottish woman had an unbelieving son who returned home from college with some new ideas and told her, "Your soul doesn't amount to anything in this vast universe." She thought it over and replied, "I agree my soul isn't worth very much, but if my soul is lost, God would lose more than I would lose. God would lose His reputation because He said that He would save me if I trusted Him." Friends, God will stand by His Word. He doesn't have to take an oath; all He needs to do is to say it, and it is truth. He wants those who represent Him down here to be that kind of a people. If they make a vow, they should stand by that vow. This kind of responsibility should be representative of the Christians in this world today.

CHAPTER 31

THEME: Judgment of Midian

Remember that we are dealing with things that pertain to the new generation which has come through the wilderness. Many of them were just little fellows when they started out. Some were grade schoolers, some were high schoolers, and some had not even been born when they started the wilderness march. God is preparing this new generation for their entrance into the Promised Land.

The Midianites, you recall, joined the Moabites in hiring Balaam to curse Israel and afterwards seduced the people to idolatry and licentiousness. The only woman named in this seduction was Cozbi, a Midianite (Num. 25:6–16). After this episode God commanded His people, "Vex the Midianites, and smite them: For they vex you with their wiles, wherewith they have beguiled you in the matter of Peor, and in the matter of Cozbi, the daughter of a prince of Midian, their sister, which was slain in the day of the plague for Peor's sake" (Num. 25:17–18).

Midian in the wilderness is a type of the world. For the child of God there is to be a spiritual separation from the world today.

JUDGMENT OF MIDIAN

We are now going into the last official acts of Moses. When we get to Deuteronomy, we will have the last private acts of Moses. One of his last official acts is this war against the Midianites.

> And the LORD spake unto Moses, saying,

> Avenge the children of Israel of the Midianites: afterward shalt thou be gathered unto thy people.

> And Moses spake unto the people, saying, Arm some of yourselves unto the war, and let them go against

the Midianites, and avenge the LORD of Midian [Num.
31:1–3].

Now God commands Moses to make war against them. He is going to
avenge Israel. They are to deal very harshly with them.

> And Moses sent them to the war, a thousand of every
> tribe, them and Phinehas the son of Eleazar the priest,
> to the war, with the holy instruments, and the trumpets
> to blow in his hand [Num. 31:6].

Moses sent out twelve thousand men to go to war—one thousand from
each tribe. The holy instruments, the articles of furniture in the tabernacle, were to go along, indicating that this was a spiritual warfare.

> And they warred against the Midianites, as the LORD
> commanded Moses; and they slew all the males.

> And they slew the kings of Midian, beside the rest of
> them that were slain; namely, Evi, and Rekem, and Zur,
> and Hur, and Reba, five kings of Midian: Balaam also
> the son of Beor they slew with the sword [Num. 31:7–8].

The kings of Midian were slain, and we note here the death of Balaam,
the prophet. God is giving them a victory over the Midianites. There is
a judgment on the Gentiles here, prior to the entering into the Promised Land. This is the same thing that will consummate the age before
Christ comes. For in the Millennium, Israel, which is having such
great problems today, will be put in the land and they will have peace.

But now there is a problem.

> And the children of Israel took all the women of Midian
> captives, and their little ones, and took the spoil of all
> their cattle, and all their flocks, and all their goods
> [Num. 31:9].

God gave them a tremendous victory—they did not even lose one man
(v. 49).

> **And Moses was wroth with the officers of the host, with
> the captains over thousands, and captains over hun-
> dreds, which came from the battle.**
>
> **And Moses said unto them, Have ye saved all the women
> alive?**
>
> **Behold, these caused the children of Israel, through the
> counsel of Balaam, to commit trespass against the LORD
> in the matter of Peor, and there was a plague among the
> congregation of the LORD [Num. 3:14-16].**

There was a great problem with the children of Israel. God had taken
them out of Egypt in one night. But it took God forty years to get Egypt
out of them. And even now, after they had been tricked into idolatry,
through the advice of Balaam to the Midianites, they still bring the
Midianite women into their camp. That is the problem with worldli-
ness. It is not wrong for us to be in the world—that is where God has
placed us—the great issue is whether the world is in us, in our hearts
and lives.

The important lesson of this chapter is that it calls for spiritual
separation from the world. Where are you walking? Do you walk in
the light? Are you in the Word of God? Are you in fellowship with
Christ? That is the important thing for the child of God.

CHAPTER 32

THEME: Reuben and Gad ask for land on the wrong side of Jordan

This chapter tells us about the half-hearted tribes. Reuben, Gad, and the half tribe of Manasseh ask for land on the wrong side of the Jordan River.

This incident has a tremendous spiritual application for us, as we consider the Jordan River as a type of the death and resurrection of Christ.

REUBEN AND GAD ASK FOR LAND ON THE WRONG SIDE OF JORDAN

Now the children of Reuben and the children of Gad had a very great multitude of cattle: and when they saw the land of Jazer, and the land of Gilead, that, behold, the place was a place for cattle;

The children of Gad and the children of Reuben came and spake unto Moses, and to Eleazar the priest, and unto the princes of the congregation, saying,

Ataroth, and Dibon, and Jazer, and Nimrah, and Heshbon, and Elealeh, and Shebam, and Nebo, and Beon,

Even the country which the LORD smote before the congregation of Israel, is a land for cattle, and thy servants have cattle:

Wherefore, said they, if we have found grace in thy sight, let this land be given unto thy servants for a possession, and bring us not over Jordan [Num. 32:1–5].

Moses is very disturbed at their request.

> And Moses said unto the children of Gad and to the children of Reuben, Shall your brethren go to war, and shall ye sit here?

> And wherefore discourage ye the heart of the children of Israel from going over into the land which the Lord hath given them? [Num. 32:6-7].

He remembers all too vividly the utter discouragement of the people when they heard the report of the men who had spied out the land almost forty years earlier.

> Thus did your fathers, when I sent them from Kadesh-barnea to see the land.

> For when they went up unto the valley of Eshcol, and saw the land, they discouraged the heart of the children of Israel, that they should not go into the land which the Lord had given them [Num. 32:8-9].

Remember this is a new generation that Moses is talking to. They were too young to remember that tragic experience, and Moses is reviewing it for them.

> And the Lord's anger was kindled the same time, and he sware, saying,

> Surely none of the men that came up out of Egypt, from twenty years old and upward, shall see the land which I sware unto Abraham, unto Isaac, and unto Jacob; because they have not wholly followed me:

> Save Caleb the son of Jephunneh the Kenezite, and Joshua the son of Nun: for they have wholly followed the Lord.

> And the LORD's anger was kindled against Israel, and he
> made them wander in the wilderness forty years, until
> all the generation, that had done evil in the sight of the
> LORD, was consumed [Num. 32:10–13].

Moses fears this young generation will repeat the failure of their
fathers.

> And, behold, ye are risen up in your fathers' stead, an
> increase of sinful men, to augment yet the fierce anger of
> the LORD toward Israel.

> For if ye turn away from after him, he will yet again
> leave them in the wilderness; and ye shall destroy all
> this people [Num. 32:14–15].

You can well understand Moses' fears here. After enduring the hard-
ships and discouragements of forty years in that terrible wilderness,
the thought of again failing to enter the Promised Land seemed too
much to risk.

> And they came near unto him, and said, We will build
> sheepfolds here for our cattle, and cities for our little
> ones:

> But we ourselves will go ready armed before the chil-
> dren of Israel, until we have brought them unto their
> place: and our little ones shall dwell in the fenced cities
> because of the inhabitants of the land.

> We will not return unto our houses, until the children of
> Israel have inherited every man his inheritance.

> For we will not inherit with them on yonder side Jordan,
> or forward; because our inheritance is fallen to us on
> this side Jordan eastward [Num. 32:16–19].

They offered to send their men of war to help the other nine and one half tribes to take the Promised Land. On this basis, Moses agreed to let them settle on the east side of Jordan. They not only agreed to do it, but we find in Joshua 12—16 that they made good their promise.

Moses warned them:

> **But if ye will not do so, behold, ye have sinned against the LORD: and be sure your sin will find you out [Num. 32:23].**

The way this is usually interpreted is, "Your sin will be found out." In other words, if you sin, you won't get by with it. You will be found out. That is not what it says at all. There are a great many sinners who get by with their sins and are never found out by anyone else.

This verse says that your sin will find you out. There will come that time when the chickens come home to roost. "Be not deceived; God is not mocked: for whatsoever a man soweth, that shall he also reap" (Gal. 6:7). I don't care who you are, or where you are, how you are, or when you are, your sins will find you out. In the way that you sin, that is the way it is going to come home to you sometime. That is the meaning of this statement, "Be sure your sin will find you out."

> **And Moses gave unto them, even to the children of Gad, and to the children of Reuben, and unto half the tribe of Manasseh the son of Joseph, the kingdom of Sihon king of the Amorites, and the kingdom of Og king of Bashan, the land, with the cities thereof in the coasts, even the cities of the country round about [Num. 32:33].**

These tribes that chose the wrong side of Jordan did not have the opportunity of crossing over the River Jordan.

We need to realize, friends, that the River Jordan does not symbolize our death. When we get to the Book of Joshua, we'll see that it teaches how we pass over into Canaan. In other words, there are two places for the child of God to live today. You can live in the wilderness

of this world and be a spiritual pauper, or you can enter into the place
of spiritual blessings, represented by Canaan. Now how can we pass
over the Jordan into the place of spiritual blessing? When we see the
children of Israel crossing over Jordan, we find two great lessons
there. The stones that were put in Jordan speak of the death of Christ.
The stones that were taken out of Jordan speak of the resurrection of
Christ. You and I get our spiritual blessings by the death and resurrection of Christ. We today are to know that we've been buried with Him
and raised with Him. We are to reckon on the fact that we are joined to
Him. We are to yield to Him on that kind of basis so that you and I can
appropriate the spiritual blessings that are ours.

The two and one half tribes did not cross the Jordan. Did this work
out to their disadvantage? Yes. Our Lord said that by their fruits ye
shall know them. When He was here on earth, one time He was trying
to get away from the crowd, "And they came over unto the other side
of the sea, into the country of the Gadarenes" (Mark 5:1). Now who are
the Gadarenes? They are the tribe of Gad, living on the wrong side of
the Jordan River. And when Jesus came to them, he found them in the
pig business, you remember. And when He healed the demon-
possessed man, the Gadarenes asked the Lord Jesus to leave their
country! They had gotten into a sad condition. This always happens to
the child of God who fails to cross Jordan and get into the Land of
Promise.

CHAPTER 33

THEME: The log of the journeys; the law of the possession of the land

Here we have a log of their journeys. We said before that we do not have a record of the happenings during their forty years of wandering, only a few isolated incidents, but here is the log of the journey, a record of the places they camped.

THE LOG OF THE JOURNEYS

These are the journeys of the children of Israel, which went forth out of the land of Egypt with their armies under the hand of Moses and Aaron [Num. 33:1].

Here are a couple of verses to show you that this is not very exciting reading.

And they removed from Haradah, and pitched in Makheloth.

And they removed from Makheloth, and encamped at Tahath.

And they departed from Tahath, and pitched at Tarah.

And they removed from Tarah, and pitched in Mithcah [Num. 33:25–28].

I'd call it pretty monotonous. We would like to know what happened there, but nothing is said about what took place.

If you went to visit a friend who had just returned from Europe, you would ask him to tell you about his trip. Suppose he said that they went to Rome, then they went to Milan, then they went to Florence, then they went into Switzerland to Lucerne, then to Zurich and to Geneva, and then into Germany into Frankfurt, and so on and on. You would want to ask him what they saw and what they did. You'd find a recital of all the places they had been a pretty boring account of their trip. That is my opinion of this chapter; it's not very interesting reading.

And yet, just as each portion of Scripture has a great spiritual lesson, so this chapter has a great spiritual lesson for us. Although this chapter is like a road map, and not interesting to read, it reveals that God noted and recorded every step that these people took. In fact, He was with them every step of the way through the wilderness march.

We sing a song today which is entitled "I'll go with Him all the way." Very candidly, I don't like it, and I think it expresses exactly the opposite viewpoint from what it should say. When I was a pastor, I used to look out on the congregation singing, "I'll go with Him all the way," and then I wouldn't see many of those people on Sunday night, or at any Bible study, or when there was any work to be done for God. I wonder how far would they really be willing to go with Him? I must confess that I have failed Him. I can't promise that I will go with Him all the way. I think we should turn that song around. He will go with me all the way, for He has said, ". . . I will never leave thee, nor forsake thee" (Heb. 13:5).

So here we have the log of their journey. Everywhere they went, every time they camped, He was with them. Frankly, they weren't going with Him. That is, their hearts were in rebellion against Him a great deal of the time. But He never left them. He never did forsake them.

This is one of the great truths of the Word of God. "I will never leave thee, nor forsake thee." Jesus said the same thing in His upper room discourse, "I will not leave you comfortless" (which is, literally, I will not leave you orphans): "I will come to you" (John 14:18). How? By sending the Holy Spirit. The Holy Spirit indwells every believer. If you are a child of God, you couldn't possibly get away from Him. He wouldn't let you go. He will go with you all the way. We may stumble, falter, and fail. We don't follow Him as we ought. But, thank God, He goes with us all the way!

THE LAW OF THE POSSESSION OF THE LAND

The chapter closes with an order the Lord gives to Moses as Israel is preparing to enter the land.

> **Speak unto the children of Israel, and say unto them, When ye are passed over Jordan into the land of Canaan;**
>
> **Then ye shall drive out all the inhabitants of the land from before you, and destroy all their pictures, and destroy all their molten images, and quite pluck down all their high places:**
>
> **And ye shall dispossess the inhabitants of the land, and dwell therein: for I have given you the land to possess it.**
>
> **And ye shall divide the land by lot for an inheritance among your families: and to the more ye shall give the more inheritance, and to the fewer ye shall give the less inheritance: every man's inheritance shall be in the place where his lot falleth; according to the tribes of your fathers ye shall inherit.**
>
> **But if ye will not drive out the inhabitants of the land from before you; then it shall come to pass, that those which ye let remain of them shall be pricks in your eyes, and thorns in your sides, and shall vex you in the land wherein ye dwell.**
>
> **Moreover it shall come to pass, that I shall do unto you, as I thought to do unto them [Num. 33:51–56].**

Here is something many folk, especially the skeptics, raise questions about. People say they think it is very cruel and unfair for the Lord to tell Israel to wipe out the inhabitants of the land, when Israel also had been disobedient. They contend that because the people in the land were such lovely folk that the Lord's wanting to put them out is indefensible. That is the way the liberal and the skeptic have been talking for years. The chances are that every liberal today is living on a piece of ground that once belonged to the Indians, and I don't see them giving back their property to the Indians!

Look at this with me for just a moment. "The earth is the LORD's, and the fulness thereof; the world, and they that dwell therein" (Ps. 24:1). This is His earth. He commands what is to be done. He told Israel to go into the land and to destroy their pictures; that is, their idols. The archaeologists are digging them up today. And they were to destroy their melted images. They were to demolish their high places. These were places of pagan and heathen worship where the vilest practices took place. The Canaanites were in a very low spiritual state. Not only were they idolators, far from the living and the true God, but promiscuity and sexual sins were a way of life and a part of their worship. As a result, the Canaanites were eaten up with venereal disease.

Our promiscuous society tries to minimize the terribleness of sexual sins. We have an epidemic of venereal disease today, a plague, and it is a grave danger. It does great injury to the human race. These disease-ridden Canaanites lived at the crossroads of the world. That land is one of the most sensitive spots that there is on earth. It is that yet today; it always has been; I think it always will be. It is a strategic land and the armies of the world have marched through that land. Trade routes of the world go through that land. The Canaanites had contact with a great number of people, and they were disseminating their loathsome diseases everywhere. So God is going to put a new tenant in the land. The Canaanites were destroying His property, and they were hurting the rest of mankind; so God is going to put them out.

Don't come to me, my friend, and say that God did not have the right to do that. It was actually an act of mercy. God destroyed the Canaanites for the sake of the oncoming generations. That is the same reason that God sent the Flood—God was preserving the future generations.

My friend, do not criticize God. Do not sit in judgment on God. We cannot realize all that is involved in any situation. One thing we do know—we will not experience peace on this earth until the rule of the Prince of Peace. Until that time, God will use nations in judgment upon other nations.

CHAPTERS 34—36

THEME: Borders of the Promised Land; cities given to the Levites; law regarding the inheritance of the land

BORDERS OF THE PROMISED LAND

This is an important chapter because it defines in unmistakable terms the extent of the land that God gave to Israel. Also it underscores the fact that God gave the land to Israel for an eternal possession. Regardless of who claims it today, that land belongs to Israel.

> And the LORD spake unto Moses, saying,
>
> Command the children of Israel, and say unto them, When ye come into the land of Canaan; (this is the land that shall fall unto you for an inheritance, even the land of Canaan with the coasts thereof:) [Num. 34:1–2].

He gives the south border:

> Then your south quarter shall be from the wilderness of Zin along by the coast of Edom, and your south border shall be the outmost coast of the salt sea eastward [Num. 34:3].

Then He points out the west border:

> And as for the western border, ye shall even have the great sea for a border: this shall be your west border [Num. 34:6].

And He establishes the north border:

> And this shall be your north border: from the great sea ye shall point out for you mount Hor: